Great Warships

Great Warships

Antony Preston

GALLERY BOOKS
An imprint of W.H. Smith Publishers Inc.
112 Madison Avenue
New York, New York 10016

A Bison Book

Published by Gallery Books
A Division of W H Smith Publishers Inc.
112 Madison Avenue
New York, New York 10016

Produced by
Bison Books Corp.
17 Sherwood Place
Greenwich, CT 06830

ISBN 0-8317-4089-2

Printed in Hong Kong

1 2 3 4 5 6 7 8 9 10

Page 1: Merchant ships in
convoy under the 6-inch guns
of HMS *Sheffield*.

Pages 2-3: The USS *New
Jersey* in the Pacific in 1983,
refuelling the frigate
Meyerkord.

Pages 4-5: The *Admiral Graf
Spee* was Nazi Germany's
representative at the
Coronation Naval Review
held for King George VI in
1937.

Contents

Introduction

Many qualities go to make a great ship: a good war record, an excellence of design, or even mere good looks. Unlike aircraft or tanks, which are remembered by general type, the bigger warships are individual and easily remembered by name.

Sailors are both superstitious and romantic, but even the most skeptical landsman cannot deny that certain ships acquire a definable 'character' which defies rational analysis. Sometimes that character is good, but equally it can be bad. Ships can become 'unlucky,' and suffer a succession of disasters throughout their active lives, while others escape disaster by a hair's breadth time after time.

Qualities of design are harder to define than character. Some ships are overtaken by events, and find themselves facing threats never envisaged by their designers, while others win remarkable victories over opponents of superior fighting power, on paper at least. Good design can at times defy definition but, as in all walks of life, bad design soon makes itself felt. Like aircraft, it is generally held that 'if it looks good, then it probably is good,' but some truly handsome ships like HMS *Hood* can be fatally flawed.

Other ships have short but violent careers, like the German commerce-raiders *Emden* and *Graf Spee*, which were both sunk within three months of the outbreak of war. Similarly the American carriers *Hornet*, *Wasp*, *Lexington* and *Yorktown* were comparatively early victims of the fierce fighting in the Pacific. We would hardly be human not to find the careers of such warships more exciting than the ships which emerged victorious in 1945, some worn-out by four or five years of hard driving and others scarcely out of the shipyard.

In an age which is dominated by giant aircraft carriers and nuclear submarines the battleship represents an almost mystical 'Golden Age' of sea power. Her awesome guns and impressive statistics continue to fascinate a generation of professional sailors and skeptical defense analysts with equal ease. Although the destructive effects of naval

Far left: Aircraft on the forward flight deck of the USS *Enterprise.*

Left: The 16-inch guns of the *New Jersey* firing at Beirut in January 1984.

Above: John Hamilton's portrayal of the D-Day bombardment on 6 June 1944, with HMSs *Warspite, Ramillies* and *Roberts* in action.

Right: John Hamilton's painting of HMS *Illustrious* under attack by Stuka dive-bombers off Malta in January 1941.

Introduction

gunnery have frequently been exaggerated, the moral effect is unquestionable. Not only does the enemy suffer but one's own side is immensely heartened by the noise of 16-inch gunfire.

For many years the building of battleships was confined to the advanced industrial nations, and efforts to transfer technology to less advanced countries were frustrated by numerous difficulties. Probably the only success outside Europe was the French and British effort to transfer technology to Japan in the late 19th century. Today Third World countries insist on such transfer of technology as a matter of course, and many sophisticated warships are built in countries with no genuine naval industrial base.

The Japanese effort to build a navy second to none in quality was continually hampered by industrial shortcomings. Before World War I Germany had technical expertise in abundance but could not match British industrial strength, any more than Japan could match America's industrial might 20 years later.

All this serves as a backcloth to the choice of ships in this book. Any choice of 10 great warships must be agonizing, for so many excellent candidates have to be excluded for lack of space.

It is hardly a coincidence that the three German ships chosen were all commerce-raiders. The *Emden*, with her air of pre-1914 chivalry, is undoubtedly the most romantic, with a dashing captain using his wits to hide his ship from her numerous enemies. Langsdorff in the *Graf Spee* retained some of the glamour of his predecessor, but her final fight off Montevideo had overtones of David and Goliath rather than a straight fight between ships of approximately similar power, while the hunt for the *Bismarck* took that process even further. The *Graf Spee* and *Bismarck* also reflect the industrial and technical challenge to German warship designers in their efforts to circumvent the restrictions of the Versailles Treaty.

The choice of the Japanese battleship *Yamato* is obvious, for in her battleship superlatives reached an ultimate limit. Everything about the design was big, but ironically her career was almost an anticlimax, a history of inactivity and abortive operations. Not so obvious is the choice of the cruiser *Mogami*, but she epitomizes even more than the *Yamato* the ingenuity of Japanese designers. Unlike the *Yamato* her career was packed with action, and right to the end she had the reputation of being a lucky ship.

The *Warspite* could hardly be missed out as the outstanding 'character' of the many ships which served in the Royal Navy. With a career spanning two world wars, including the greatest set-piece sea battle since Trafalgar, *Warspite* qualifies as a great warship. The much younger *Illustrious* won a similar place in the affections of the Fleet Air Arm by playing the main role in the great air attack on Taranto and then surviving a terrible attack off Malta. Like the *Warspite* she developed a reputa-

tion for eccentric behavior, not unconnected with her severe battle damage.

The cruiser counterpart of HMS *Illustrious* was the *Sheffield*, a veteran of every important naval action in the European Theater. Unlike the carrier she survived into the 1960s, playing her part in the post-World War II navy after a facelift. Her design reflected a classic British compromise between the need for endurance and a need to match the gunpower and speed of the *Mogami*. As such she marked a new British approach to cruiser design which culminated in the *Belfast* and *Fiji* Classes.

To choose out of the numerous American ships which distinguished themselves is difficult, but in aircraft carriers and carrier tactics the US Navy excelled over all others, so the USS *Enterprise* is the natural choice. Not only did she have an outstanding career in the Pacific but her design embodied all that was developed into the even more battleworthy *Essex* design. Last of all is the *New Jersey*, representative not only of the finest class of American battleships ever built but also a ship currently in service. She and her sisters of the *Iowa* Class have been returned to active duty in the 1980s, a full three decades after everyone had consigned the battleship to the history books. The *New Jersey* has fought no major battles but to have been recommissioned three times since the end of World War II is sufficiently unusual to justify her inclusion among these 10 great ships.

Above: The after high-angle gun director of the cruiser *Sheffield*, with the triple 6-inch turrets trained to starboard.

Right: Swordfish torpedo-bombers on the forward flight deck of the aircraft carrier *Illustrious* in the spring of 1942.

Overleaf: The *Emden* in pursuit of a merchant ship, the classic role of the commerce-raiding cruiser.

1. SMS Emden

The story of the German light cruiser *Emden* is a classic of naval warfare. Her short career at the start of World War I has overtones of chivalry, audacity and romance which are at odds with the later savagery of U-Boat warfare. It is also the story of one ship against the mightiest navy in the world, enjoying a short but brilliant career.

The expanding Imperial German Navy gave a lot of thought to the design of cruisers. From 1898 a series of classes emerged, each one a step toward achieving a balance between an 'overseas' or commerce-raiding cruiser and a 'scout' to work with the battle fleet, reconnoitering and providing protection against torpedo boats. With the *Gazelle*, laid down in that year, the balance between the two types was achieved for the first time.

A series of step-by-step improvements through six more designs produced a series of cruisers displacing 33–3500 tons, armed with 10 105mm (4.1-inch) single guns and capable of 23–4 knots. In the 1905–06 Program two more cruisers were funded as replacements for two old cruisers. They were given the provisional names *Ersatz Comet* and *Ersatz Pfeil*, but on launch they became *Dresden* and *Emden*. Armament was similar to preceding ships of this type of *kleine Kreuzer* but, in keeping with Marineamt policy of introducing improvements, they were given for the first time a thin (80–100mm) strake of side armor along the waterline, to keep out light shells. Previous German light cruisers had relied solely on a protective deck, but new lighter steel enabled a limited amount of side

Right: SMS *Emden* docked for scraping and painting.

Below: The *Emden* at sea, probably on her trials in 1909.

protection to be adopted. Another improvement was to give the *Dresden* two sets of the new Parsons steam turbine, whereas her sister retained the well-tried 3-cylinder triple-expansion engines. Both ships were coal-fired, so the 400 tons of coal normally carried in side bunkers afforded additional protection against underwater damage.

The *Emden* was laid down in April 1906 at the Imperial Dockyard in Danzig. She was launched in May 1908 and joined the Fleet in July 1909. After brief service in home waters she was decommissioned in December 1909 but recommissioned at the beginning of April the following year, being assigned to the Cruiser Squadron for service overseas. She left for the Far East via Cape Horn, and arrived at Tsingtao in September 1910.

14

SMS Emden

By the summer of 1914 SMS *Emden* had served nearly four years with the Cruiser Squadron on the Far Eastern Station, with the armored cruisers *Gneisenau* and *Scharnhorst* (flying the flag of Vice Admiral Maxmilian von Spee) and the light cruisers *Leipzig* and *Nürnberg*. Since 1913 she had been commanded by Kapitänleutnant Karl von Müller (soon to be promoted to Fregattenkäpitan). He had served on the staff of the Reichsmarineamt and was a popular and able officer.

During the last weeks of peace the *Emden* found herself the only cruiser left on station; the other ships of her squadron had left on a cruise in the South Pacific or were *en route* to other stations. Von Müller was the senior naval officer on station and certain responsibilities automatically devolved upon his shoulders. He had, for example, the responsibility for mobilizing logistic support, and had to supply his admiral with Intelligence about enemy movements.

When he received news of the impending hostilities on 31 July von Müller immediately took steps to prepare his ship for commerce-raiding in the Far East, in the hope that this would prevent Allied warships from concentrating on Tsingtao. So smooth was the transition to a war footing that the *Emden* left harbor the same evening. On 2 August her captain learned that Germany was at war with Russia and the following day he learned that France had joined Russia, so the ship was headed for the Korean Straits.

The first victim of the *Emden* was a Russian steamer, the *Rjasan*, which tried to escape but was forced to surrender after 12 shots were fired. She was sent with a prize crew back to Tsingtao, where she was refitted as an auxiliary cruiser and renamed *Kormoran*.

The attitude of Japan was crucial to German plans in the Far East. If she remained neutral Spee planned to attack British shipping in the Indian Ocean, but when Japan made it clear that she would join the Allies the plans were hurriedly changed. To avoid a clash with a powerful Japanese squadron Spee decided to leave the area, heading for the coast of South America. When von Müller heard of the new plans he protested that at least one light cruiser should be detached to keep the British busy while Spee's squadron was crossing the Pacific. If this did not happen, he argued, weeks would pass with no damage inflicted on the enemy.

Spee, as we know, crossed the Pacific to score a victory at Coronel, and then suffered annihilation at the Falklands a month later, but the *Emden* was given permission to proceed to the Indian Ocean, where she was to do far more damage than the main squadron. The Indian Ocean was crucial to the British war effort, and many ships were at sea on the trade routes from the Far East to the Suez Canal. Coal supplies would be crucial but von Müller reckoned on capturing sufficient colliers, and there were numerous secluded anchorages where his ship could coal without being interrupted.

The plan was to concentrate on the trade routes between Singapore and Colombo, and Colombo and Aden. Von Müller's plan was to keep out of sight for as long as possible and then make a fast raid to achieve maximum surprise. He therefore traversed the Malay Archipelago via the Moluccas and the Banda Sea. In the Palau Islands he coaled from the collier *Markomannia*, then headed for the Lombok Strait, passing the powerful armored cruiser HMS *Hampshire* in the night. To puzzle any observers the ship rigged a dummy funnel to turn her into a four-funnelled ship, more like a British cruiser.

The British China Squadron under Vice Admiral Jerram was now hunting for the *Emden*. His forces included the Royal Navy cruisers *Minotaur*, *Hampshire* and *Yarmouth*, the armed merchant cruisers *Empress of Asia*, *Empress of Japan* and *Himalaya*, the French cruiser *Dupleix* and the Japanese cruisers *Ibuki* and *Chikuma*. But when the *Emden* reached the Bay of Bengal on 5 September shipping had resumed its regular schedules in the hope that it would be 'business as usual.' To make the task even easier for the *Emden*, large convoys of troopships were heading for Aden and the Suez Canal, and while the Allied warships in the East Indies were committed to escorting them less important shipping was unprotected.

On 10 September the cruiser found her second victim, the Greek collier *Pontoporros*, which was promptly taken over as a prize. During the next three days five British merchant ships were intercepted; four were sunk while one was retained to accommodate all the *Emden*'s prisoners. Not one of the ships had managed to send a radio message, but von Müller wisely decided to move out of the

Above: The *Emden* at Tsingtao in August 1914, with the armored cruisers *Scharnhorst* and *Gneisenau* for the last time.

Above right: Vice Admiral Maximilian von Spee, commander of the Far Eastern Squadron.

Above far right: Captain Karl von Müller, who took command of the *Emden* in 1913.

Above: Shell holes in the oil
tanks at Madras after the
Emden's bombardment.

West of Colombo *Emden* sank two British
steamers on 24 September, and captured the collier
Buresk the following day, as well as sinking two
more steamers before heading for the Andaman
Islands. The effect of all this on maritime trade was
catastrophic; shipping movements all but ceased
from 14 September to 2 October and the value of
exports from India fell by over 60 percent.

After coaling in the Maldive Islands the *Emden*
went south to Diego Garcia, where the news of the
outbreak of war had not been received. In blissful
ignorance the British outpost there treated the
Germans hospitably and allowed the cruiser to
take on coal and to scrape marine growths from the
bottom of the hull.

After capturing five more ships von Müller
decided to make another raid, this time on Penang.
Emden arrived off the harbor at about 0300 hours
on 29 October, with the dummy fourth funnel
rigged to confuse lookouts. As she glided into the
harbor at 18 knots a string of lights was seen on the
starboard bow, about 1200 yards away. As the
mystery ship drew closer she was identified as a
Russian light cruiser, the *Zhemchug*, but clearly her
lookouts had seen nothing.

When only 300 yards away the *Emden* fired a
torpedo from the starboard underwater tube and
opened fire with every gun that could bear. The
torpedo hit abreast of the *Zhemchug*'s after funnel,
causing a huge explosion and her sides were riddled
by 105mm shells. All the victim could do was
return the fire with one gun, but in the confusion no
hits were scored on her attacker. A second torpedo
hit level with the bridge, apparently setting off a
magazine explosion, and when the smoke cleared
only the *Zhemchug*'s mast was above the water.

area into the Bay of Bengal. There he sank two
more ships. When the presence of a German commerce-raider was finally confirmed there was some-
thing like panic in shipping circles. All movements
stopped and coastal lights were extinguished.

The *Emden* proceeded to cause further conster-
nation by bombarding Madras. At about 2000
hours on 22 September she approached the port at
high speed, and when she was some 3000 yards
from the pierhead switched on searchlights and
started to shell the oil-storage tanks. Two caught
fire and another three tanks were damaged, while a
steamer was hit and minor damage caused to the
harbor installations. As usual *Emden* escaped unscathed, for once again the cruisers hunting her
crisscrossed her track without coming close enough
to make an interception.

SMS Emden

Von Müller turned north and increased speed to get clear of any other enemy warships which might be in the vicinity, but even at this critical juncture he could not resist adding another prize to his total. While he was putting a prize crew aboard, his lookouts warned that an unidentified warship was approaching from the northwest.

This was the small French destroyer *Mousquet*, which put up a brave fight but was overwhelmed by gunfire and sank within minutes. A second French destroyer was avoided easily and the raider escaped by hiding in a rain squall. After coaling from the *Buresk* she headed for the Cocos Islands, where von Müller planned to cut the submarine cable and destroy the wireless station before going on to harass shipping on the Australian routes.

She approached the small island on which the cable and wireless station was located during the night of 8–9 October, arriving off Port Refuge at 0600 hours. With clear weather and no ships in sight the Germans hoped to have several hours in which to wreck the installation and cut the cable, and as soon as she anchored a landing party of two officers, six petty officers and 38 sailors went ashore in the ship's boats.

Events did not go exactly as planned. The radio operators on the island had already sent a signal 'Emden here' when they spotted the dummy funnel, and although the ship's radio operators were jamming the transmissions, another signal went off, 'Unidentified ship off entrance.' The wrecking of the radio station proceeded as planned but cutting the cable took longer than expected, and while the shore party was still engaged in this task a warship was heard on the radio, calling the shore station.

The *Emden*'s radio operators reported that the mystery warship was transmitting from a distance of 250 miles but they were badly mistaken; the Australian cruiser *Sydney* was just over 50 miles away, escorting a large convoy of troopships to Colombo. Although the second message from the

Cocos had not got through the first one had, and the *Sydney* had immediately left her convoy at high speed.

At 0900 hours the German lookouts sighted what was taken to be a cloud on the horizon but within 30 minutes it was recognized as coal smoke from a warship steaming at high speed. It was too late for the landing party to rejoin the ship, and *Emden* went into battle without several key personnel on board.

Above: **Prisoners from the *Emden* exercising on board a British armored cruiser, on their way to captivity.**

Left: Kapitänleutnant von Mucke, second in command of the *Emden*, led the landing party on an epic voyage back to the Red Sea.

Far left: One of the *Emden*'s guns in place ashore at Port Refuge.

THE DAILY MIRROR, Monday, December 21, 1914.

HOW WE SANK THE EMDEN: PHOTOGRAPHS

The Daily Mirror

CERTIFIED CIRCULATION LARGER THAN ANY OTHER DAILY NEWSPAPER IN THE WORLD

No. 3,482.   Registered at the G.P.O. as a Newspaper.   MONDAY, DECEMBER 21, 1914   One Halfpenny.

THE END OF THE ·EMDEN: THE LAST PHASE OF GERMANY'S MOST FAMOUS DESTROYER OF BRITISH COMMERCE.

The end of the action. Note the Emden's side and guns blown away on the port quarter-deck.

First boat-load of Emden prisoners.

H.M.S. Sydney just after she had sunk the Emden.

Taking the wounded on to H.M.S. Sydney.

These are the first photographs to reach England of the sinking of the Emden, the famous German corsair of the sea which destroyed so much valuable British commerce, by H.M.S. Sydney, of the Australian Navy. As will be seen from the photo- graphs of the two ships taken at the conclusion of the engagement, the Emden proved no match for the Sydney. The German cruiser was shattered by the shell fire of the Sydney, but the British ship came out of the fight practically unscathed.

Above right: A public hungry for war news was given a feast when the dramatic pictures of the *Emden*'s sinking were published late in December 1914.

The ship's luck had deserted her, for her adversary was faster and better armed than *Emden*. Approaching from the north the *Sydney* turned straight for the *Emden*, denying her any chance of escape. At 9500 yards, a range at which the 105mm shells could not penetrate *Sydney*'s waterline armor, *Sydney* quickly found the range, but the *Emden* scored two hits, one on the forward range-finder which did not explode, and a second on the after control position which wounded several men.

Although the *Emden* gamely tried to close the range to improve the chance of scoring a crippling hit, the *Sydney*'s 6-inch guns began to cause havoc. A shell destroyed the radio shack, another killed the forward gun crews, and the fire-control system was knocked out. The fighting efficiency rapidly fell off; firing orders had to be given by voicepipe, and when the steering broke down the ship was steered by hand. The forward funnel collapsed and casualties mounted.

SMS Emden

Fire was slackening because of the casualties among the exposed gun crews and ammunition parties, and von Müller turned the ship to bring the disengaged side into action, but to no avail. His only hope now was a torpedo attack, but a single shot at 4500 yards missed (the *Sydney*'s torpedo also missed about this time). By 1045 hours the ship was a shambles, with the foremast and the remaining funnels knocked down. Attempts to close the range were repeatedly frustrated by her opponent's superior speed and gunpower.

Von Müller's last act of defiance was to run the ship ashore on a reef, to prevent her from being captured. Sadly, when the *Sydney* asked by signal if the ship had surrendered no answer was given (the signal books had been destroyed), and she opened fire once more, until white flags were seen. The losses were disproportionate. The *Emden* lost 134 killed and 65 wounded, out of a total complement of 376, while the *Sydney* had 3 killed and 13 wounded.

Although von Müller and the survivors were taken prisoner the landing party escaped capture because the *Sydney* departed at once to rejoin her convoy, not realizing that people had been left ashore. Their subsequent adventures rival the exploits of the cruiser, for they managed to make their escape all the way back to Turkey.

Realizing that he might have to wait for months, and then almost certainly would be taken prisoner, the first lieutenant, von Mücke, ordered the men of the landing party to prepare an old sailing schooner for sea. Although warned that the 97-ton *Ayesha* was unseaworthy, the Germans set sail for Padang that night. From there she sailed to Hodeida, then occupied by Germany's Turkish allies, who transported the sailors overland to Constantinople (Istanbul). There von Mücke and his men reported to Admiral Souchon, the man who had taken the battle-cruiser *Goeben* and the cruiser *Breslau* into Turkish waters in August 1914.

During her epic cruise the *Emden* steamed 30,000 miles and sank 16 British merchant ships totalling 70,825 tons gross. In addition she took three prizes and let four British ships go after inspection. Her commander had acted boldly and energetically, and had succeeded in causing great inconvenience to the Allies. Scores of ships were involved in the hunt for the *Emden*, from battleships down to destroyers. *Emden* had achieved her primary objective, to tie up as many ships of the enemy's fleet as she could.

Her sister *Dresden* fought with Spee's squadron at Coronel, and escaped the carnage of the Battle of the Falklands by hiding among the islands of Tierra del Fuego. On 14 March the light cruiser *Glasgow*, the armored cruiser *Kent* and the armed liner *Orama* found her lying off the Chilean island of Mas a Fuera. The British ships were forced to keep their distance while negotiations were conducted between the Germans and the Chileans, but when it became clear that the German negotiator,

THE MIGHT OF BRITAIN, by GENERAL FULLER, D.S.O.

29th DECEMBER, 1939

THE **WAR** WEEKLY

No. 10

3D.

A NEWNES PUBLICATION

HOW WE BEAT THE *GRAF SPEE*

This dramatic picture, specially drawn for "War Weekly," represents the running fight between three of our cruisers and the German pocket battleship, the *Graf Spee*, which, badly battered, fled to seek refuge in a neutral port.

GLORY OF OUR NAVY, ARMY, AIR FORCE, TANKS AND GUNS IN EIGHT WONDERFUL PAGES OF PICTURES

Above left: Officers and ratings of the *Emden* received a hero's welcome on their arrival at Constantinople in June 1915.

Left: The Emden's landing party preparing for a leisurely return to the ship from Direction Island. The schooner *Ayesha* is in the background.

Above: The epic cruise of the *Emden* and the bravery of von Spee's squadron had a compelling effect on the German Navy, which hoped to repeat its success with 'pocket battleships.'

Lieutenant Wilhelm Canaris (later Chief of German Counterintelligence), was merely playing for time the British ships opened fire and the *Dresden* was promptly scuttled to avoid capture.

For over 40 years the rusting wreck of the *Emden* remained on the reef, but it was finally broken up by Japanese scrap merchants in the 1950s. All that is left to commemorate her last fight is the bow and foremast of HMAS *Sydney*, preserved in Sydney, Australia.

2. HMS Warspite

The claim of the *Warspite* to be the most famous British battleship rests on her unique achievement of playing a major role in both world wars. She was heavily engaged in the Battle of Jutland in 1916 and went through some of the most arduous campaigns in World War II, suffering severe damage on several occasions.

She was the second of a new class of battleships ordered under the 1912–13 Estimates, which set new standards of firepower and speed. The *Queen Elizabeth* Class came about because of dissatisfaction with the concept of the lightly armored battle-cruiser. What was wanted was a 'fast wing' of the battle fleet, capable of independent action yet well-protected against the heaviest fire. The arrival of Winston Churchill on the scene as First Lord of the Admiralty in 1911 gave further impetus to the cause, for he was sympathetic to the idea of outstripping the German Navy by a big margin. There was also pressure to raise gun caliber from 13.5 inches to 15 inches, as the latest American and Japanese capital ships would have 14-inch guns, and it was rumored (falsely) that the next German battleships would follow suit.

There were, however, major drawbacks to the adoption of such a large caliber at short notice. Designs for a twin 15-inch gun mounting existed but the guns had not been manufactured. It is normal to build and 'prove' (fire experimentally) at least one gun before a design is accepted into service, but if this course had been followed there would have been an unacceptable delay in laying down the 1912 Program ships. The choice seemed to lie between building ships with less-powerful guns than foreign rivals or sending them to sea with novel and untried weaponry.

Britain's naval armaments industry was at the height of its power, enjoying a uniquely successful partnership with the Admiralty. The Armstrong gun foundry at Elswick on the Tyne had been designing and supplying heavy gun mountings for many years, and the Director of Naval Ordnance (DNO) was confident that their experience would result in a highly successful gun and mounting. With the DNO's assurance, the Board of Admiralty gave the go-ahead to the new ships, with the proviso that one of the first batch of 15-inch guns should be hurried to completion four months ahead of the rest, to permit proof-firing, from which range tables and other information could be compiled. As the whole object was to steal a march over the German Navy the new gun was to be referred to as the '14-inch Experimental.'

As originally conceived the new ships would have been merely larger versions of the previous class, with five twin 15-inch (two turrets at either end of the ship and one amidships) but the greater power and weight of broadside of the 15-inch armament persuaded the Admiralty that the long-discussed 'fast wing' might be achievable. By dropping the fifth turret, space could be found for sufficient extra boilers to boost speed from 21 to 25

Above left: HMS *Warspite* after her first modernization in the 1920s, with her antitorpedo 'bulges' visible.

Left: The *Warspite*'s mascot.

Above: The Malaya, like the *Warspite* and the rest of the *Queen Elizabeth* Class, had her elegant twin funnels trunked into one to reduce smoke interference.

Right: HMS *Valiant* in the late 1920s.

knots. The weight of shells in an 8-gun broadside of 15-inch was considerably heavier than a broadside of 10 13.5-inch, so the faster ship would still be more powerful.

One more innovation remained. By adopting oil instead of coal as the fuel, the ships would achieve their speed more efficiently, with the same endurance for less weight. The weight saved could be put into more protection, to offset the sacrifice of the protection afforded by coal bunkers sited between the armor and the working areas of the ship. Refuelling would also be a far simpler and cleaner procedure. In many ways this was the most far-reaching decision, for it committed Great Britain to the acquisition of large holdings in the Middle East oilfields.

With the details of the design settled it was possible to place orders for four ships under the 1912–13 Estimates: *Queen Elizabeth*, *Warspite*, *Valiant* and *Barham*. Then the Federated Malay States offered to pay for a fifth unit, and to commemorate the gift the ship was named *Malaya*. A

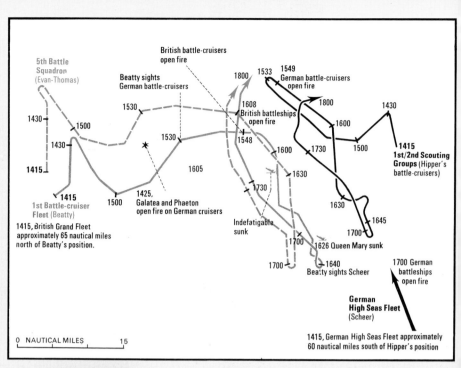

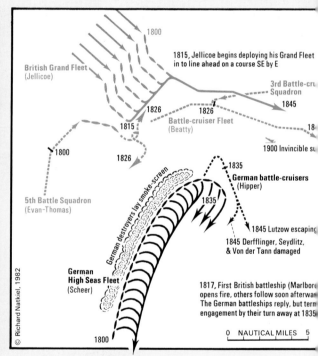

sixth ship, to be named *Agincourt*, was ordered under the 1914–15 Estimates but she was cancelled on the outbreak of war.

The *Warspite* was laid down at the end of October 1912 at Devonport Dockyard in Plymouth. Her launch took place on 26 November 1913 and she was commissioned in March 1915. With World War I already eight months old the new battleship was hurried through her gunnery trials in five days and in mid-April she arrived at Scapa Flow, where she joined the 5th Battle Squadron. There she remained, with the rest of the class joining, until in January 1916 the squadron included all five of the class.

Although the Grand Fleet's existence at Scapa Flow was monotonous, with occasional sorties in

Far left: Damage to the *Warspite*'s starboard side after a collision with her sister HMS *Barham* in December 1915.

Left: The Battle of Jutland.

Above: Shipwrights repairing one of the *Warspite*'s shell hits after Jutland in May 1916.

Right: Admiral Sir David Beatty, who commanded the battle-cruisers and the 5th Battle Squadron at Jutland.

the hope of catching the German High Seas Fleet at sea, the *Warspite*'s career was not without incident. In September 1915 she ran aground, and only a month after she emerged from dock she was back again after colliding with her sister *Barham*.

When the day came for the High Seas Fleet to give battle, off the Jutland Bank on 31 May 1916, HMS *Warspite* was lying third in line in the 5th Battle Squadron, headed by the flagship *Barham* and the *Valiant*, with the *Malaya* astern. The squadron had been moved to Rosyth as a temporary reinforcement to the Battle Cruiser Force of Vice Admiral Sir David Beatty, while three of his ships were away on gunnery exercises. With warnings from Intelligence sources that the Germans were putting to sea, Beatty was anxious not to frighten them off, and the four *Queen Elizabeth* Class were stationed 10 miles astern.

When the German battle-cruisers were sighted the flagship *Lion* passed the sighting report to the *Barham* by flags which could not be seen properly, and failed to repeat the report by lamp, so Admiral Evan-Thomas was late in joining the action. However, after an interval of 20 minutes his force was able to begin firing at the rear of the German line. When Beatty's ships turned north, once again a signalling lapse left the battleships in ignorance of the fresh course, and a delay of 14 minutes occurred before the 5th Battle Squadron hauled round. The Germans found the 15-inch fire very accurate, and their guns were outranged.

In the next phase of the battle the two main fleets came into action. Evan-Thomas could not get to his proper battle station ahead of the Grand Fleet, so altered course to join the rear of the battle line. While this turn was in progress the *Warspite*'s helm jammed, and she started to turn circles. She was comparatively close to the most powerful German battleships, and seven of them opened a heavy fire on her. She suffered at least 13 heavy (11-inch and 12-inch) hits and five from 5.9-inch shells. She had already been hit twice in the previous action, making 15 major shell-hits in all.

One of the shells pierced the upper armor belt, wrecked the port feed tank and caused flooding in one of the port engine-rooms. One of the 5.9-inch shells hit the left-hand 15-inch gun in 'Y' turret aft, bulging the barrel and putting it out of action. Another shell burst on the forecastle deck, sending its flash through a small hole into the 6-inch gun battery and igniting some cordite charges, but the fire was put out.

The ship was afloat, but with so much damage she was not fit for further combat, and was ordered to proceed independently to Rosyth with two destroyers as an escort. She docked in the Firth of Forth. Repairs took about seven weeks and she did not rejoin her squadron until 23 July. By now she was getting the reputation of being unlucky, for on 24 August she suffered serious damage in a second collision, with the *Valiant*. In June the following year she had a minor collision with a destroyer, but for the rest of the war she and the rest of the squadron maintained their vigil at Scapa Flow.

The *Queen Elizabeth*s were the mainstay of the battlefleet in the 1920s, and they served in the Mediterranean Fleet and the Atlantic Fleet (later renamed the Home Fleet). The *Warspite* was given

a partial modernization from November 1924 to April 1926, but much more drastic updating would be needed if the ship was to go to war for the second time in her career.

In March 1934 she was drydocked at Portsmouth to begin a complete rebuilding. To provide a margin for improving protection against both heavy shells and bombs it was necessary to replace her machinery with much lighter turbines and boilers, saving 1600 tons. With the hull opened up the opportunity was taken to remove the 15-inch turrets, to overhaul them and increase maximum possible elevation from 20 to 30 degrees. This, combined with new shells, increased range from 23,400 to 32,200 yards.

When the *Warspite* emerged in March 1937 her appearance had changed completely. The original layout, with two elegant tall funnels, had been changed in the 1920s by trunking the forward funnel into the after one to reduce smoke interference, but now she had a massive block of bridgework, a single large funnel and a hangar amidships big enough to accommodate two floatplanes.

In June 1937 she recommissioned for service with the Mediterranean Fleet as the new flagship. Her reputation for bad luck continued to dog her; while carrying out a full-caliber shoot she narrowly missed a passenger liner which had strayed into the target area, and at Malta she inadvertently fired her eight-barrelled pompoms into the crowded city of Valetta. Fortunately neither accident harmed anybody, but it was not until the ship was well into World War II that the 'hoodoo' was exorcized.

The ship's first action occurred in April 1940, when she was sent to support the Norwegian campaign. In a uniquely daring counterstroke Admiral Whitworth took the battleship and nine destroyers

Above: The newly reconstructed *Warspite* in July 1937. The tricolor stripes on 'B' turret are for identification in the vicinity of Spanish waters, to avoid bombing by Republican and Nationalist forces.

Below left: A cheer from the ship's company as the new flagship leaves for the Mediterranean in January 1938.

Right: HMS *Warspite* refuelling the Australian destroyer *Nestor* in the Indian Ocean.

into Narvik Fjord to hunt out the German destroyers which had captured the port some days earlier. The *Warspite*'s 15-inch guns crippled several destroyers, while her Swordfish floatplane kept track of enemy movements throughout the battle. Taking a battleship into such confined waters was a risk, but the end result was the destruction of the entire German force.

On her return to the Mediterranean she hoisted the flag of Admiral Cunningham, the new Commander in Chief of the Mediterranean Fleet, and under his inspired leadership the *Warspite* was destined to win immortality. She was soon in action against the Italians, in the Battle of Calabria on 9 July 1940. During this brief skirmish the *Warspite* scored a devastating hit on the battleship *Giulio Cesare*, putting four boilers out of action and causing 115 casualties. This hit, scored at a range of 26,500 yards, established a record for naval gunnery against a moving target which has never been equalled.

After this rough handling the Italian Fleet showed even less enthusiasm for battle, but in March 1941 the two sides' capital ships clashed again. Italian forces were at sea to support their land forces in Greece, when in the afternoon of 28 March a Fleet Air Arm torpedo-bomber from the carrier *Formidable* torpedoed the battleship *Vittorio Veneto*. That evening another hit was scored on the *Pola*, one of three heavy cruisers sent to help the battleship.

As things turned out, the battleship made her escape but during the night Cunningham's battleship force, the *Warspite*, *Valiant* and *Barham*, ran into the heavy cruisers *Pola*, *Zara* and *Fiume*. The Italians were ill-equipped for night fighting, and were taken completely by surprise when illuminated by British searchlights. Only 10 seconds after the destroyer *Greyhound* turned on her searchlight the *Warspite*'s turrets opened fire with a six-gun salvo. At only 2900 yards, five or six hits were observed and the target burst into flames. As the arcs opened all eight guns fired in the next broadside. Target was shifted to the next target, another heavy cruiser, and most of the third broadside hit her too, causing fires to break out. After that two of the escorting destroyers came under fire. Within ten minutes the entire action was over, leaving the *Pola*, *Fiume* and *Zara* and two destroyers sunk.

The Battle of Cape Matapan (known to the Italians as the Battle of Gaudo Island) was the first decisive action at sea since World War I, and although small numbers of ships were involved it had important consequences. The shock to the Italian Navy was severe, and they made no further attempt to hinder the passage of British reinforcements. Nor, when fortunes were reversed, could they bring themselves to interrupt the evacuations from Greece and Crete. It also confirmed the moral ascendancy which the Mediterranean Fleet had gained over the Italians.

Warspite was severely damaged during the

HMS Warspite

evacuation of Crete. On 22 May she was hit by a 500-pound bomb which hit abreast the funnel on the starboard side. It blew a large hole in the forecastle deck, blew a twin 4-inch antiaircraft gun mounting overboard and started fires in the starboard 6-inch battery.

Despite No 3 boiler room being abandoned when it filled with smoke and fumes the flagship remained in action, and did not return to Alexandria for another two days. While in dock she was near-missed by a 1000-pound bomb which damaged the antitorpedo 'bulge,' but on 25 May she left for the United States. At Bremerton Navy Yard she was repaired and overhauled, sailing to join the Eastern Fleet in the Indian Ocean early the following January.

After a comparatively uneventful stay with the Eastern Fleet she was sent home in March 1943. On 17 June she sailed for Gibraltar with part of the amphibious forces assembling for Operation Husky, the landings in Sicily. Although attacked by German aircraft she was not harmed, and her bombardments were successful. On 10 September

Above: A conference in Captain Kelsey's quarters aboard the *Warspite* before the Walcheren landings.

Left: Warspite's First Lieutenant, with the main 15-inch gun director behind.

Above right: Warspite's after 15-inch guns firing at Catania during the Sicilian landings in July 1943.

Right: The map shows *Warspite*'s position during the Normandy bombardment.

she escorted the pride of the Italian Navy on its way to surrender at Malta, and it must have given her crew satisfaction to see her old enemies the *Vittorio Veneto* and *Giulio Cesare*.

Although the Italians wanted no more of the war the Germans were determined to carry on, and so the Salerno landings on the Italian mainland went ahead as scheduled. Once again *Warspite*'s accurate gunnery provided invaluable support to the troops ashore, but on the third day her luck ran out. Just after 1400 hours, having completed a bombardment, she engaged a group of Fw 190 fighter-bombers. However, they were only a feint for another attack; three radio-controlled bombs were launched and guided by three bombers from a height of 20,000 feet. The bombs approached at a height of 6–8000 feet and when overhead dived almost vertically.

The three hits came close to sinking the ship. The first hit the boat deck and penetrated all the decks, exploding in the double bottom under No 4 boiler room. The second detonated about 6 feet off the starboard side, abreast of No 5 boiler room, while the third hit the sea and exploded without causing further damage. With five out of the six boiler rooms flooded and a number of key compartments damaged by shock the old battleship was in bad way. Her main machinery was, however, intact, and using steam from the single boiler room still working she managed to crawl clear, but at 1500 hours the boilers ran short of feedwater and had to be shut down. Electric power was gone, along with radar, radio and hydraulic power for the main armament. In all she had 5000 tons of water on board, was drawing nearly 40 feet of water and had a list of 4 degrees to starboard.

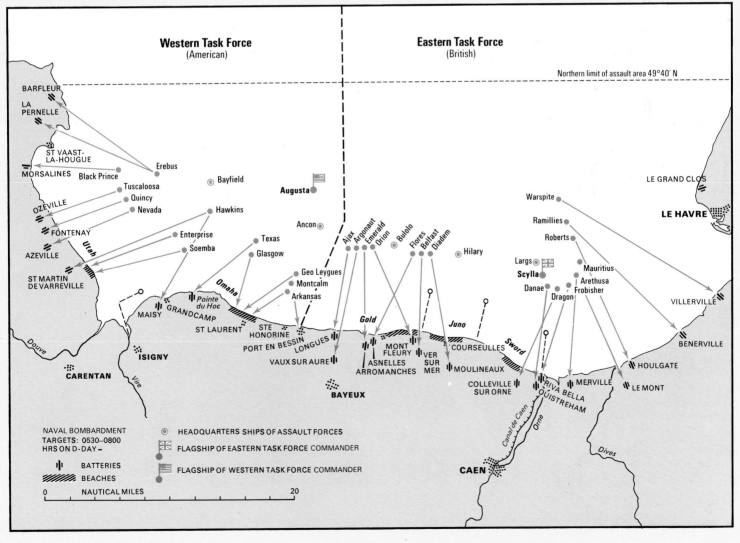

Western Task Force
(American)

Eastern Task Force
(British)

Northern limit of assault area 49°40′ N

BARFLEUR

LA
PERNELLE

ST VAAST-
LA-HOUGUE

MORSALINES
Black Prince
Erebus

Tuscaloosa
Quincy
OZEVILLE
Nevada
Hawkins

FONTENAY

Enterprise
AZEVILLE
Soemba

Utah

ST MARTIN
DE VARREVILLE

◉ Bayfield

LE GRAND CLOS

Augusta ⚑

Ancon ◉

Texas
Glasgow

Geo Leygues
Montcalm
Arkansas

Omaha

Pointe
du Hoc
MAISY
GRANDCAMP
ST. LAURENT

STE
HONORINE
PORT EN BESSIN
LONGUES

VAUX SUR AURE

ISIGNY

Douve

CARENTAN

Vire

BAYEUX

Ajax
Argonaut
Emerald
Orion
Bulolo
Flores
Belfast
Diadem

◉ Hilary

Gold

MONT
FLEURY
ASNELLES
ARROMANCHES

VER
SUR
MER

Juno
COURSEULLES

MOULINEAUX

COLLEVILLE
SUR ORNE

Warspite

Ramillies

Roberts

Largs ◉ 🇬🇧
Scylla

Danae
Dragon

LE HAVRE

Mauritius
Arethusa
Frobisher

VILLERVILLE

BENERVILLE

Sword

RIVA BELLA
OUISTREHAM

HOULGATE

MERVILLE
LE MONT

Canal de Caen

Orne

CAEN

Dives

NAVAL BOMBARDMENT
TARGETS: 0530–0800
HRS ON D-DAY —

⬛ BATTERIES

▨ BEACHES

0   NAUTICAL MILES   20

◉ HEADQUARTERS SHIPS OF ASSAULT FORCES

🇬🇧 FLAGSHIP OF EASTERN TASK FORCE COMMANDER

🇺🇸 FLAGSHIP OF WESTERN TASK FORCE COMMANDER

HMS Warspite

Two US tugs took her in tow to Malta, but while passing through the Straits of Messina she became ungovernable and eventually it took six tugs to tow her sideways. At Malta she was patched up for the long journey home, where she was needed for the Normandy landings. However as a very old and hard-worked ship she was not considered worth a full repair, and even the works carried out at Rosyth in March 1944 were limited. 'X' turret never worked again and No 4 boiler room was not repaired.

After rendering heroic service off the D-Day beaches, the *Warspite* was sent to Rosyth to replace her badly worn 15-inch guns, but on 13 June, a day after leaving Portsmouth, she set off a magnetic mine. The explosion jammed her rudder and the main and auxiliary machinery suffered shock damage. Despite this severe damage the ship, now known familiarly as the 'Old Lady,' reached Rosyth under her own steam. There she was patched up once more, but only three shafts could turn, so her speed was reduced to 15.5 knots.

By now very much a geriatric patient, the *War-spite* continued to carry out bombardments, against Brest and Le Havre and finally Walcheren in November 1944. On 1 February 1945, almost 30 years since hoisting her commissioning pennant for the first time, she was placed in Category C Reserve.

The old ship was slowly stripped of useful fittings such as light antiaircraft guns, and at the end of July 1946 approval was given to sell her for scrap. Many people who had served in her thought that she should have been preserved as a war memorial but on 12 March 1947 she left Portsmouth in tow for the breakers. Then on 23 April it was learned that she had broken her tow in a gale off the Cornish coast, and was hard aground in Prussia Cove. So strong was the 'character' of the *Warspite* that many former crewmen claimed that the ship would never allow herself to suffer the humiliation of being cut up for scrap. Ships do develop distinct identities, and the *Warspite* had a decidedly quirky character. No ship can cheat the breakers, but the *Warspite* strung the process out as long as she could, and the last remains were not removed from Prussia Cove for another nine years.

Above: The *Warspite* laid up in Spithead in 1946, with her sisters *Queen Elizabeth* and *Malaya*. The age of the battleship seemed to be at an end, but within five years a new lease of life had begun.

Right: In April 1947 the stripped hulk that had been HMS *Warspite* broke her tow and ran aground in Prussia Cove, Cornwall. It took nine more years to remove her last remains.

3. Admiral Graf Spee

At Versailles in 1919 the victorious Allies forced on the defeated German Empire a humiliating treaty, with the avowed intention of ensuring that Germany could never again be a major military power. The naval clauses were framed to restrict the new Reichsmarine to a coast-defense role, and much thought was given to ways of preventing the construction of ocean-going commerce-raiders.

Specifically, the Versailles Treaty forbade the building of warships larger than 10,000 tons, or with guns greater than 11-inch (28cm) caliber. This, it was hoped, would limit the Reichsmarine to nothing more powerful than a coast-defense battleship. Even numbers would be limited to six, to be built when existing obsolete pre-Dreadnought battleships reached their age limit.

Many designs were considered, starting with a straight attempt to comply with the Versailles Treaty, but mounting national resentment at what were regarded as shackles imposed by jealous rivals gave the naval administration encouragement to try to achieve the formula first promulgated by Admiral Fisher 25 years earlier: a warship 'stronger than anything faster and faster than anything stronger.'

The answer lay in a combination of new technology and outright duplicity. By adopting diesel propulsion and electric welding it would be possible to save a great deal of weight, but even by concentrating the armament in two triple turrets it was not possible to achieve an armament of six 11-inch guns, $3\frac{1}{2}$- to 4-inch armor protection and a speed of 26 knots within the treaty limit of 10,000 tons. Like the Japanese, the Germans had no hesitation in accepting that the new design would contravene the Treaty, and merely declared that the ships displaced 10,000 tons. As always international disarmament treaties not subject to inspection proved unenforceable.

The first ship was laid down in February 1929 and was given the proud name *Deutschland* when launched. Her effect on public opinion was tremendous, both inside and outside Germany. To the German public she was proof that the Versailles Treaty could be outflanked by German ingenuity (the choice of name fostered this sense of national prestige), while the foreign press dubbed her a 'pocket battleship.' Although the other signatories protested that Germany was guilty of evading the provisions of the treaty, in the absence of proof that the *Deutschland* exceeded the tonnage limit they could only admit that the ship fell within the prescribed limits. Only France protested that the ship was clearly intended to attack her shipping, and insisted on the right to build a fast capital ship in reply. As so often in the 1930s, Germany's bluff had paid off, and the Americans and British gave in.

A month after the launch of the *Deutschland* a second *Panzerschiff* (armored ship) was laid down, and she entered service in November 1934 as the *Admiral Scheer*. The third of an intended total of

Left: Sailors parade on the quarterdeck of the *Admiral Graf Spee* in Wilhelmshaven in January 1936.

Below: The first *Panzerschiff*, the *Deutschland*, in Hamburg in 1935. She differed in many details from her sisters *Graf Spee* and *Scheer*.

Right: The massive triple 11-inch (28-cm) gun turrets and tower bridge contributed much to the reputation of the *Panzerschiff* design.

six was laid down in October 1932, launched in June 1934 and was commissioned in January 1936 as the *Admiral Graf Spee*. By this time Hitler had abrogated the Versailles Treaty and there was no political limit on naval expansion, so construction of *Panzerschiffe* was stopped in favor of true capital ships displacing a nominal 26,000 tons.

Although not the first naval diesel engines, the eight double-acting 9-cylinder MAN diesel engines were an unusually powerful installation by warship standards, and never tried before in such large ships. Not only did they achieve power on less weight than steam turbines of the equivalent power but they were also much more economical. At her economical speed of 18 knots a *Panzerschiff* could hope to cruise 9000 nautical miles – less than the designers hoped but roughly twice what an equivalent steam-powered ship could achieve on the same tonnage of fuel.

There were other advantages to diesel engines which made them particularly suited to commerce-raiding cruisers. They make comparatively little smoke, so enemy warships were less likely to spot them at long range. They also provide rapid acceleration, giving a *Panzerschiff* a good 15 minutes' start in making a getaway. Therein lay the rationale for the design; they were not intended to

fight their opposite numbers, but to roam the high seas in search of undefended merchant ships, using guns and torpedoes to deter weaker warships from trying to engage.

The armor protection, which was slightly increased in the *Admiral Graf Spee* (usually shortened to *Graf Spee*), was angled to increase its resistance to armor-piercing shell. There was also a 45mm-thick deck, while the gun turrets and the control tower were well protected. In 1938 the ship was given another secret advantage; she received the first operational radar set in the German Navy. The *Dé Té-Gerat* had a distinctive 'mattress' antenna fitted to the main rangefinder on the roof of the control tower. It was a cumbersome piece of equipment which could determine range quite accurately but not bearing, and its main use was for surveillance at night or in poor visibility.

On her completion in 1936 the *Graf Spee*

Right: The *Graf Spee* at Almeria during the Spanish Civil War. After her sister *Deutschland* (from whose deck this photograph was taken) was bombed the German ships shelled Republican targets as a reprisal.

Below: The *Graf Spee* dressed overall for the May 1937 Coronation Naval Review at Spithead.

Admiral Graf Spee

became the Fleet Flagship, and with her sisters was employed on what was euphemistically termed 'maritime control' during the Spanish Civil War. These duties included actions against Republican (Communist) forces. She returned home in 1938 for a short refit, and was in home waters before the outbreak of World War II.

The C in C, Admiral Raeder, had devised an ocean strategy in which the three *Panzerschiffe* had a major role to play. He was determined to avoid the strangulation which Germany had suffered from the British blockade in World War I, and hoped to use surface raiders, in conjunction with the U-Boats, to disrupt the British convoy system. To avoid being caught by the blockade Raeder wanted as many ships as possible to be at sea before the outbreak of war, and in accordance with his plans the *Graf Spee* sailed on the evening of 21 August 1939. Eleven days later she made a rendezvous with her supply ship *Altmark* southwest of the Canaries.

Ten days later, while supplies were being transferred from the *Altmark*, the ship's floatplane reported an unidentified ship heading their way. The floatplane was recovered and both German ships got under way quickly, avoiding the heavy cruiser *Cumberland* by a short margin. In fact the *Graf Spee* had not yet begun commerce-raiding as her orders had not come through; Hitler still hoped for a negotiated peace with Britain and France after the speedy collapse of Poland. Not until 26 September 1939 was permission received to attack shipping, and even then attacks had to comply with the so-called Prize Regulations, which meant ensuring the safety of crews.

Four days after her narrow escape the *Graf Spee* found her first victim. At 1300 hours on 30 September lookouts sighted a steamer which altered course and tried to get away. Captain

Langsdorff ordered the floatplane to be launched, and the pilot succeeded in forcing the victim to heave to. She turned out to be the SS *Clement*, and she was soon scuttled, but not before her master had sent a radio message to the Admiralty and the machinery had been put out of action.

Langsdorff knew that the *Clement*'s last message would bring warships to the scene, so he left the coast of South America and headed for the Cape of Good Hope, where he knew there would be many targets. To confuse the British he painted dark stripes on the front and sides of the control tower to give the impression of a tripod mast. At 0700 hours on 5 October another steamship was sighted by the lookouts, and Langsdorff altered course to approach her bows-on. When less than 2000 yards away he ran up a string of flag-hoists ordering the ship to heave-to and not to use her radio. This time it was the SS *Newton Beech*, which succeeded only in transmitting a weak signal before German board parties reached the radio room. They also found copies of the Admiralty's secret orders and prescribed routes.

The *Newton Beech* was not sunk, as Langsdorff wanted to get rid of his prisoners. She remained in company, and in spite of two narrow escapes avoided detection. Her original SOS message had been heard by another merchant ship, which had passed it on to HMS *Cumberland*, but the cruiser had been unwilling to break radio silence as it was not preceded by the 'RRR' prefix. Then four days later the carrier *Ark Royal* sighted her but the prizemaster pretended she was the American SS *Delmar* and the ship was allowed to proceed.

The next victim, the SS *Ashlea*, was also deceived by the false tripod mast. She was captured just after 0825 hours on 7 October, having been boarded before she could send any SOS signal, as the *Ashlea*'s master thought he had encountered a

Above: The *Admiral Scheer*, seen during the Spanish Civil War, was very similar to the *Graf Spee* in appearance.

Above right: The SS *Ashlea* is sunk by a torpedo fired by the *Graf Spee*.

Above far right: Captain Hans Langsdorff, commanding officer of the *Graf Spee*.

Above: The SS *Doric Star,*
another victim of a torpedo.

French warship. After transferring usable stores and provisions Langsdorff ordered the *Ashlea* sunk. A search of her radio room had revealed a logbook of ships' positions, and this further convinced Langsdorff that he must keep changing area.

The *Newton Beech* was a liability, being very slow, and next day she was sunk after transferring her prisoners back to the *Graf Spee*. On 10 October the next victim fell to the raider. The SS *Huntsman* was taken in by the false tripod mast, and managed to get only one brief distress signal sent off. Langsdorff was a remarkably humane man, and would not sink the *Huntsman* because her crew could not be accommodated on board his own ship. He therefore put a prize crew aboard with instructions to steam to a prearranged meeting point.

These three captures had all taken place north of St Helena, so Langsdorff decided to rejoin the

Altmark on 15 October, and the two ships then met up with the *Huntsman* next day. He wanted to head back towards the Cape route and then into the Indian Ocean. On 22 October, off Walvis Bay on the coast of South West Africa (now Namibia), he encountered the motor ship *Trevanion* and sank her. Once again Langsdorff's bluff worked, and the *Graf Spee* got within 350 yards before revealing her nationality. Although under fire the victim managed to put out a distress call, but once again it was garbled, missing out the name *Trevanion* and giving a garbled estimate of her position.

Next morning the *Graf Spee*'s radio operator picked up a message from the Royal Navy's Simonstown base, calling on all ships to repeat a distress call made the previous day. Two ships complied, each giving wrong positions, but the second one happened to coincide with the *Graf Spee*'s position. It was high time to leave the area, for the Allies now had the carrier *Ark Royal*, the battle-cruiser *Renown* and the French battle-cruiser *Strasbourg* in the South Atlantic, looking for the mystery raider.

Refuelling and revictualling was completed from the *Altmark* west of the Cape on 28 October, and the *Graf Spee* now headed for the waters south of Madagascar. Langsdorff was actually laying a false trail to disguise his intention to get back to Germany, for after steaming 30,000 miles (one-and-a-half times the earth's circumference) the diesels were showing signs of wear and tear.

The raider had little luck at first. Early on the morning of 14 November off Lourenco Marques (now Maputo) she sighted a small Dutch coaster but had to let her go as she could not be boarded in the rough weather. Next day at noon *Graf Spee* caught the small tanker *Africa Shell* and sank her with gunfire, but left the area rapidly after being sighted by a Japanese steamer. During a week-long

Admiral Graf Spee

Record of the Graf Spee's activities

30 Sept	Clement sunk
5 Oct	Newton Beech boarded
7 Oct	„ „ sunk
7 Oct	Ashlea sunk
10 Oct	Huntsman boarded
17 „	„ „ sunk
22 Oct	Trevanion sunk
14 Nov	Holland sighted
15 Nov	Africa Shell sunk
16 Nov	Mapia stopped
2 Dec	Doric Star sunk
3 Dec	Tairoa sunk
7 Dec	Streonshalh sunk

refit and replenishment period alongside the *Altmark* the ship's crew erected a dummy gun turret in 'B' position and a dummy second funnel to further confuse enemy observers.

With the short refit over it was now time to try to return to Germany. On 2 December she sighted smoke on the horizon and flew off the Arado floatplane to investigate. Now Langsdorff's luck changed, and when the floatplane failed to return he ordered his victim to be stopped by gunfire. At a range of 14 miles the 11-inch turrets could not correct fall of shot fast enough to prevent the ship, the SS *Doric Star*, from sending an 'RRR' message, with the crucial word 'battleship' added. She was sunk and that night the *Graf Spee* left the area to throw the hunters off the scent.

Next morning revealed a new victim, the steamer *Tairoa*, and on the evening of 7 December she met her last victim. The *Streonshalh* was taken without resistance, and after taking off her crew the raider sank her. A bag of confidential documents was recovered; it revealed that a small convoy would shortly be leaving the River Plate so Langsdorff decided to try his luck in that area.

Events were moving to a climax, for a Royal Navy hunting group, Force 'G,' was also moving into the River Plate area. Commodore Harwood RN had under his command the heavy cruiser *Exeter*, the light cruiser *Ajax* and her sister from the Royal New Zealand Navy HMNZS *Achilles*. In addition the heavy cruiser *Cumberland* was refitting at Port Stanley in the Falkland Islands.

During the night of 12–13 December the *Graf Spee* was patrolling some 300 miles east of the River Plate. At about 0530 hours lookouts sighted two mastheads on the starboard bow, and Langsdorff ordered the *Graf Spee* to turn toward the mystery ship, apparently under the impression that she was one of the convoy he was looking for. At 0552 hours the *Exeter* was seen and identified but the two single-funnelled cruisers in company were at first mistaken for destroyers.

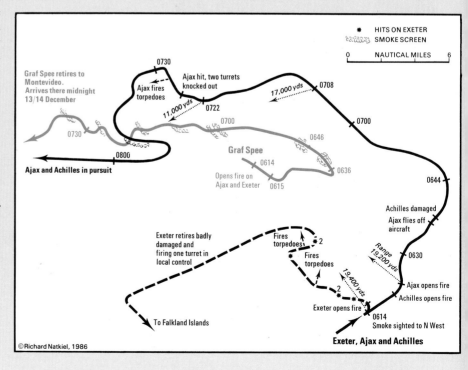

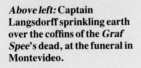

Above left: Captain Langsdorff sprinkling earth over the coffins of the *Graf Spee*'s dead, at the funeral in Montevideo.

Above: The wrecked forward 8-inch gun turrets of HMS *Exeter*, after the battle at Port Stanley in the Falklands, where she carried out emergency repairs.

There was no point in trying to escape as the British ships had a handsome margin of speed, and so the *Graf Spee* cleared for action and increased to full speed. *Exeter* herself did not identify her opponent as a *Panzerschiff* until 0616 hours, and one minute after that both 11-inch turrets opened fire on the *Graf Spee*.

On paper Harwood's force was at a severe disadvantage, badly outranged by the *Graf Spee*'s guns, but his ships were experienced and had exercised for such an encounter. Standing orders

Admiral Graf Spee

dictated the use of speed to retain the tactical advantage and to offer widely dispersed targets to the enemy's fire control. This also conferred the advantage of each cruiser using 'flank marking' to spot each other's fall of shot at long range.

The *Exeter* bore the brunt of the German fire, and was soon badly damaged. An 11-inch shell wrecked 'B' turret and caused many casualties on the bridge. After an hour only 'Y' turret was still in action, and the ship was 3 feet down by the bows, with a 7–10 degree list to starboard. Her plight would have been worse had the *Ajax* and *Achilles* not repeatedly rushed into range, fired a few salvoes of 6-inch shells and then retreated under cover of smokescreens.

The *Graf Spee* had been hit twice by the *Exeter*, and a further 14 times by 6-inch shells. Although she was not disabled the cumulative effect was serious. The repeated changes of target were too much for her fire control to handle, and each time it was necessary to waste fire on ranging shots. At 0700 hours even the battered *Exeter* returned to the battle, firing from her after turret, and the exasperated *Panzerschiff* was forced once more to shift

target. The *Ajax* took severe punishment but the *Graf Spee* had been roughly handled and Langsdorff broke off the action. His ship had suffered 36 dead and 59 wounded. The forecastle was holed, making a winter trip through the North Atlantic hazardous. Another hit had destroyed the fuel and lube oil filtration plant, making a major machinery breakdown likely. With these considerations in mind Langsdorff decided to put into neutral Montevideo, where he could repair the damage.

British diplomatic pressure forced the Uruguayan authorities to limit the German ship's stay to 72 hours, and each hour brought retribution closer. Skilful propaganda suggested that powerful forces were close at hand, but in fact the only reinforcement for Harwood was the *Cumberland*, which arrived on the night of 14–15 December to relieve the *Exeter*.

Langsdorff became more and more pessimistic, and it should not be forgotten that his ship had fired two-thirds of her ammunition. At last he made his decision, and at 1820 hours on 17 December he and a picked group of 40 officers and men took the ship to sea, followed by the steamer *Tacoma* carry-

Above: The wreck of the *Graf Spee*, ablaze after scuttling charges had been detonated by her crew.

Right: The wrecked base of the after triple 11-inch gun turret of the *Graf Spee*.

Right: The British Ambassador to Uruguay, Eugen Millington-Drake, meets Commodore Harwood in Montevideo after the battle.

Below right: Captain Langsdorff is buried by his men in Buenos Aires.

ing the rest of the crew. An hour later she hove-to outside territorial waters, and as the sun went down a series of explosions tore the *Graf Spee* apart and left her burning for two days.

The Germans were interned in Argentina next day, but early on 20 December Captain Hans Langsdorff shot himself in a hotel room. His reason for committing suicide remains obscure; perhaps knowledge of the fate which might be waiting for him in Germany, perhaps a last protest against the High Command's orders which forbade him to give battle, even against inferior odds.

For the British the Battle of the River Plate was of course a great fillip to morale. At a time when the naval war was not going well, the 'David and Goliath' conflict reaffirmed public faith in the Royal Navy. It also demolished the myth of the 'pocket battleship,' which clearly could be brought to battle by much smaller cruisers, and showed that Hitler's Kriegsmarine had not managed to exorcise the ghosts of Scapa Flow. To quote a modern historian, the German Navy still felt that whenever it went to sea it was 'trespassing on the Royal Navy's preserve.'

4. Mogami

The Imperial Japanese Navy (IJN) produced some remarkable warships in its headlong rush to offset American and British numerical superiority, and no group demonstrates Japanese ingenuity better than the four *Mogami* Class. They were built as 'light' cruisers (having a maximum gun caliber of 6.1 inches [155mm]), but were rearmed and converted to 'heavy' cruisers (armed with 8-inch [200mm] guns) in time for World War II. All four played a leading role in the Pacific war and out of the four the *Mogami* fought hardest of all.

To understand the tortuous process of Japanese cruiser design it is necessary to go back to 1930. The signing of the London Naval Treaty in that year limited the IJN to a total of 108,400 tons (standard) of 'A' type heavy cruisers and 100,450 tons of 'B' type light cruisers. The completion of the latest ships, the four *Takao* Class, would use up the total for 'A' type cruisers, while the 'B' category tonnage already totalled 98,415 tons. Fortunately four light cruisers were already over the legal age limit and two more would reach that limit in 1935 to 1936. By juggling figures it was possible to plan for other replacements, and the total replacement tonnage rose to 50,955 tons.

Out of this total the planners estimated that the IJN could build four 8500-ton light cruisers and two 8450-tonners. Orders for the first four were placed between 1931 and 1933 at an estimated cost of 24,830,000 yen. As Second Class Cruisers they were given names of rivers: *Mogamigawa*, *Mikumagawa*, *Suzuyagawa* and *Kumanogawa*, with the suffix *gawa* dropped.

Like all Japanese warship designs of the period, the specification set difficult, almost impossible, targets. First, the ship was to be armed with no fewer than five triple 6.1-inch gun mountings, 12 24-inch torpedo tubes plus antiaircraft guns but, as an added complication, the design must permit the ships to be rearmed with twin 8-inch guns after the expiry of the naval treaties or in a case of national emergency. Protection of the magazines

Above: The *Mogami* steaming on her full-power trials in the Bungo Strait in the spring of 1935.

Left: Launching the *Suzuya*, third of the *Mogami* Class, in 1936.

Right: The *Suzuya* during fitting-out, with the foundations of the bridgework and the tripod foremast visible.

Below: Forecastle and forward triple 6.1-inch gun turrets of the *Kumano*, last of the four *Mogami* Class to be completed.

was to be against 8-inch gunfire, although the machinery had only to be resistant to 6-inch gunfire. Speed was to be an astounding 37 knots, and endurance was to be 8000 nautical miles at a speed of 14 knots.

The design parameters were very similar to the 10,000-ton 'A' type heavy cruisers, so asking the design team to repeat them in a hull displacing 15 percent less proved almost impossible, even before the various departments of the Naval Staff started to request additional equipment. Even the widespread use of electric welding to save weight could not prevent the standard displacement from creeping upward to 9500 tons.

Just after the first two of the class, *Mogami* and *Mikuma*, had been launched in the spring of 1934 the Navy Board received a most alarming report. On 12 March that year the torpedo boat *Tomozuru* had capsized during the annual maneuvers, and the official enquiry revealed damning evidence of inadequate stability in all the latest classes of warship.

Several measures were taken to improve the stability of the new cruisers, including a smaller superstructure, provision for seawater ballasting and a reduction of height between decks. Other changes were introduced at the insistence of the Naval Staff, including triple torpedo tubes instead of twin ones and new heavier antiaircraft guns, pushing weight up again.

Mogami's sea trials started in March 1935, and she was soon in trouble. Transverse stability was acceptable but during her high-speed runs (without catapults, main fire-control directors, after anti-aircraft guns and so on) frames and side stringers were distorted and fuel tanks began to leak through loosened plating. Side plating at the bow was buckled by wave action and the hull was distorted, causing the gun turrets to jam on their roller paths.

After docking and repairs at Kure Navy Yard the *Mogami* recommissioned in June 1935, and with her sister *Mikuma* took part in the autumn maneuvers. During a typhoon which struck the fleet east of Miyako both of the new cruisers again suffered deformation of the hull. In the *Mogami* numerous electrically welded joints ruptured, mainly in the forward part of the hull, and once again training of the forward turrets was impaired.

The Fourth Fleet Incident, as the event was officially known, led to a much more profound reassessment of design standards. *Suzuya*, the third of the class, had her trials stopped and she joined *Mogami* and *Mikuma* in reserve, while work on the unlaunched *Kumano* was also stopped. The hull was strengthened, and 'blisters' were added externally to offset the 1000 tons of extra weight. By this time the Japanese government had announced its refusal to sign the Second London Naval Treaty, and so the go-ahead was given to rearm the *Mogami* Class with 8-inch guns while their defects were being cured.

When the *Mogami* rejoined the Fleet in April 1940 she displaced 14,000 tons and was now a

heavy cruiser, armed with 10 8-inch guns in twin turrets. As a unit of Sentai 7, she joined her sisters in a brief show of force against the French in Indochina in January–July 1941, but rapidly deteriorating relations with the United States soon gave the IJN more serious matters to worry about. On 16 November the *Mogami* embarked fuel and ammunition at Kure and four days later she and two sisters left to rendezvous with the flagship *Kumano*, which was flying the flag of Rear Admiral Kurita.

With the 12 older heavy cruisers, Sentai 7 formed the backbone of the fleet which carried out the 'First Stage Operations,' the landing operations in Malaya, British Borneo, Sumatra, Java, Burma and the Andaman Islands. The four *Mogami* Class also took part in the successful raid into the Bay of Bengal and were responsible for sinking the heavy cruiser USS *Houston* and the Australian light cruiser *Perth* in the Battle of the Java Sea. During the action off Banteng Bay on 28 February the *Mogami* and *Mikuma* sank the two ABDA cruisers with 8-inch gunfire and torpedoes, but a salvo of six 'Long Lance' torpedoes fired by *Mogami* overran the target and sank a Japanese minesweeper and four transports.

Mogami and the rest of Sentai 7 returned to Kure toward the end of April, having completed five months of arduous steaming and major fighting, but without suffering any damage to themselves. What the Japanese termed the 'Second Stage Operations,' the move against Midway, was now getting underway, and the four ships arrived at Guam on 28 May. On the night of 5 June, while some 90 miles away from Midway, the four cruisers were making an emergency turn to port to avoid an American submarine when the *Mogami* rammed the *Mikuma*. Both cruisers were damaged and while making their way slowly westward they were spotted by an SBD aircraft from the USS

Top left: Mogami (nearest camera) and her sisters *Mikuma* and *Kumano* in Ise Bay in the summer of 1938.

Left: The *Suzuya* in 1935. Her trials were stopped as soon as the *Mogami*'s design faults became known.

Above: Midway Island in November 1941, with Easter Island in the foreground.

Right: Japanese bombers score a direct hit on the USS *Yorktown* during the Battle of Midway.

Mogami

Left: The *Mikuma* lies a smoking ruin, dead in the water after bomb hits during the closing stages of the Midway battle.

Below: The *Mogami* soon after her commissioning.

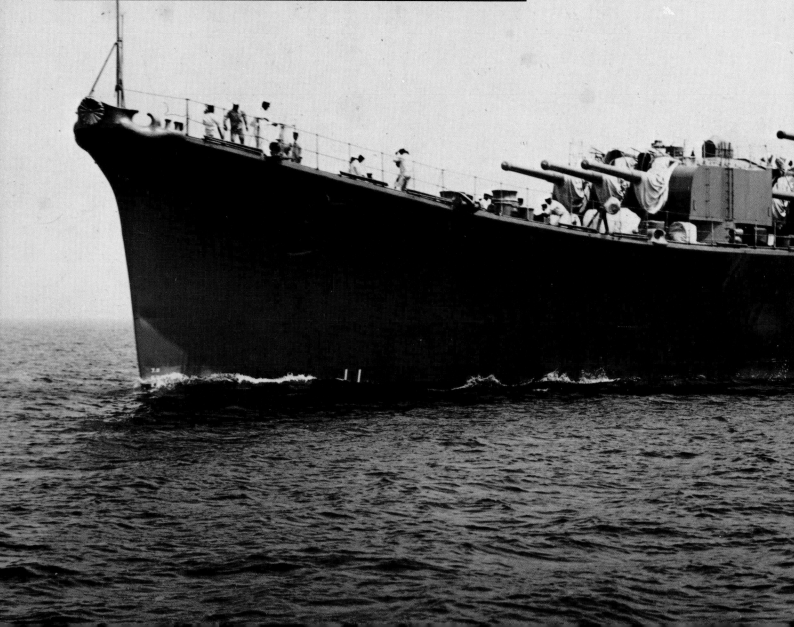

Enterprise. Between 0645 and 1145 hours they were attacked by three waves of SBDs. The *Mikuma* was so badly damaged that she had to be abandoned, but the *Mogami,* in spite of being hit five times and suffering nearly 200 casualties, succeeded in rescuing 240 survivors and getting back to Truk.

The battered cruiser took 10 months to repair. During her rebuilding she was radically altered to an 'aircraft cruiser,' with No 4 and No 5 8-inch turrets replaced by a hangar, flight deck and catapults to enable her to operate 11 reconnaissance floatplanes. In her new guise she was recommissioned at the end of April 1943 and rejoined Sentai 7, with her surviving sisters *Kumano* and *Suzuya,* at Truk. In November she was damaged during an air strike on Rabaul by planes from Task Force 38, and had to return to Kure for five months of repairs.

The war was going very badly for Japan now, and the strategy of waiting for the US Navy to expose itself to attrition was not working. During her repairs *Mogami* was given more antiaircraft guns to defend against the ever-increasing air threat. A sign of the growing desperation of the high command can be seen in the use of the newly repaired *Mogami* for carrying supplies for the army to Singapore in March 1944. From there she went to Lingga and on to Tawi Tawi, where forces were assembling for the 'A-Go' operations in the Marianas.

The *Mogami* escaped unscathed from the disastrous Battle of the Philippine Sea in June, and was sent back to Kure for another round of modifications to her antiaircraft armament. This time she received radar, which was just becoming available to the IJN in sufficient numbers, but this refinement was not to save her from the onslaught of American airpower.

It was the *Mogami*'s misfortune to be awarded a leading role in the 'Sho-Go' plan which resulted in the titanic series of battles known as the Battle of Leyte Gulf. She was to form part of Rear Admiral Nishimura's force, which included the battleships *Fuso* and *Yamashiro*. Their mission was to force their way through Surigao Strait to reinforce the main attack on the Allied amphibious forces off Samar, and their misfortune was to run into a well-prepared force of US battleships and to be the losers in the last battleship versus battleship action of World War II.

On October 24 the *Mogami* was strafed by machine-gun fire and 5-inch rockets by fighters from the carrier *Enterprise* while steaming through the Sulu Sea. Just after midnight, while passing southwest of Limasawa Island the Japanese task group was attacked unsuccessfully by PT-Boats, two of which each fired a torpedo at the *Mogami*. Her luck held and she was able to drive off the PT-Boats with searchlight-controlled gunfire.

Later piecemeal attacks by PT-Boats were also beaten off without damage but now the Japanese ships were coming under fire from destroyers at the northern end of Surigao Strait. At 0350 hours the *Mogami* came under fire while she was making a turn to port. She was hit by two 8-inch shells, one of which knocked out No 2 turret while the other started fires. Five minutes later she fired four 24-inch Model 93 oxygen-driven torpedoes from her starboard tubes and turned rapidly to the south. At 0402 hours she was hit again by heavy shells, probably fired by the USS *Portland*, and Captain Toma was killed on the bridge, along with most of the personnel stationed there.

With many casualties, and steering manually, the heavily damaged cruiser attempted to escape southward but at about 0430 hours she collided with the heavy cruiser *Nachi*. Although the damage from the collision was only superficial she was ablaze and ready-use ammunition was beginning to explode. Before crewmen could jettison the torpedoes, five exploded, increasing the carnage amidships. Everyone in No 1 and No 3 engine-rooms had been killed by blast or fire, and heat forced the evacuation of No 2 engine-room. With only one engine-room working she could only run on one propeller shaft, but at 0500 hours full rudder control was restored. Her ordeal was not over, for at

Left: The *Mogami* (top) and a *Fuso* Class battleship maneuvering under air attack in the Sulu Sea during the Battle of Leyte Gulf.

Right: The already damaged *Kumano* turns turtle on 25 November 1944 after being hit by four bombs and five torpedoes.

Right: The *Kumano*, sister of the *Mogami*, just before sinking after an attack by US carrier aircraft in Colon Bay.

Below: The hybrid carrier/ battleship *Ise* under fire off Cape Engano during the Battle of Leyte Gulf.

0530 hours she came under fire from three American cruisers, the *Louisville*, *Denver* and *Portland*, at a range of about 18,000 yards. She fired back and managed to shake them off but in the five minutes' firing she had been hit by 20 8-inch and 6-inch shells. At 0550 hours another PT-Boat was driven off, and finally at 0614 hours she made contact with the *Nachi*, rejoining the Second Strike Force about three-quarters of an hour later.

With the destroyer *Akebono* escorting her and the fires now under control it seemed that the *Mogami* might escape after all, but at 0830 hours her run of luck ended. Her remaining steam turbine broke down; she was drifting helplessly about half an hour later when she was detected by strike aircraft from Task Group 77.1. Two minutes after the attackers peeled off to attack she was hit by two 500-pound bombs on the forecastle.

Realizing that the ship was doomed the surviving senior officer gave the order to flood the forward magazines, but the flooding valves for No 1 magazine had failed. The gunnery officer gave the order to abandon ship at 1047 hours, and the *Akebono* came up on the port side to take off the survivors. About two hours later the destroyer fired a torpedo at the *Mogami*, which hit amidships.

Mogami

Even after all she had endured the *Mogami* seemed unwilling to go, and she did not finally roll over and sink for another 20 minutes. Her casualties totalled 192 officers and men.

Her sisters did not long survive her. The *Suzuya* was also a participant in the Leyte Gulf battles, but as part of the force which attacked the amphibious force off Samar. At dawn on 25 October she was damaged by a near-miss from a bomb during an attack by 10 aircraft of Task Group 77.4.3. With only one shaft turning and speed reduced to 20 knots she was a sitting duck for air attacks, and just over three hours later she was hit by a strike of 30 aircraft, and this time she was left a blazing wreck by a near-miss which started a fire among the above-water torpedo tubes. The fire set off not only the torpedoes in the tubes but all the reloads, and the ship was abandoned about three hours later.

The *Kumano* suffered the rare fate of being hit by a torpedo from an American destroyer during the surface action off Samar, when a 21-inch Mk 15 was fired at her from a distance of about 7500 yards by the USS *Johnston*. Despite this damage and subsequent near-misses from air attacks as she withdrew through the San Bernardino Strait, the cruiser limped on. Three 500-pound bomb hits failed to stop her in the Sibuyan Sea, and she finally reached Manila two days later.

Her damage was repaired in remarkably quick time, and on 3 November she was ready for sea, although her hastily repaired boilers could only drive her at 15 knots. Next day she left in company with a convoy bound for Takao, but two days later she was attacked by the US submarines *Guitarro*, *Bream*, *Raton* and *Ray*. Although three of the four American submarines claimed hits, out of 23 21-inch torpedoes fired, only two hit. These blew away the newly repaired bow and flooded the engine-rooms. In spite of this damage *Kumano* was taken in tow by a naval auxiliary and reached Santa Cruz Harbor in Luzon. There she was sunk by four bombs and five torpedoes on 25 November, capsizing to port in shallow water.

The remarkable degree of damage suffered by the *Mogami* and her sisters underlines the contradictions of Japanese warship design. The early history of the class cast grave doubts on stability and showed clear evidence of defective welding and even hull weakness, suggesting a design unsuited to withstand damage. However, battle experience showed exactly the opposite. The Imperial Japanese Navy's designers achieved their results by methods which excited nothing but contempt from Western navies, but the unorthodox approach often produced spectacular successes.

Postwar examination of Japanese records revealed that the IJN staff had laid down a policy which stressed that each design should be approached with the minimum of reference to previous designs. The sole criterion, in theory at least, was that each class should be superior in every respect to the latest foreign designs. This meant, inevitably, a high degree of risk, and there were, as have been seen, some spectacular failures. Starting with the experimental light cruiser *Yubari*, Captain Hiraga and his assistant Lieutenant Commander Fujimoto pioneered ultralight construction. Armor was worked in longitudinally, dispensing with the need for plating behind it. The distinctive 'wavy' deck was adopted to provide maximum longitudinal strength without incurring a weight penalty. It was a costly form of construction but the IJN planners were not trying to build cheap cruisers.

The war service of the *Mogami* and her sisters shows how hard they fought and the damage sustained by both *Mogami* and *Kumano* ranks them equal with any contemporary cruiser's record of battle damage. The Japanese planners were wiser than their American counterparts in foreseeing the usefulness of floatplanes in providing long-range reconnaissance; time and again floatplanes sighted hostile forces or reconnoitered target areas. The Japanese also correctly assessed the importance of

Above: The *Mogami* after being rebuilt with triple 6.1-inch mountings.

Right: The Grumman F4F-4 Wildcat was the standard US Navy fighter in 1942-3.

torpedoes; even without the 'Long Lance,' the misty conditions frequently encountered in the Pacific gave torpedo-armed cruisers an important tactical advantage.

Up to the Battle of Midway the IJN cruisers were deployed conventionally, using their high speed and firepower to screen battleships and carriers. After the US landings on Guadalcanal the cruisers were used to screen the convoys reinforcing the Japanese garrison, and in a series of fiercely-fought night actions their unique qualities came into their own. But in the long run American radar counterbalanced the Japanese superiority in weaponry and tactics and losses became unbearable.

The *Mogami* epitomizes the Japanese dilemma. Should the IJN have built larger numbers of more cost-effective ships or were they right to build to the highest standards possible? The short answer is that the Japanese could never match the United States in industrial capacity, so all they could hope to do was to match quantity with quality. That decision may have been wrong, but it produced some of the most remarkable cruisers ever seen, and their fighting record is second to none.

Above: A US Navy destroyer's crewman notches up another 'kill' during the fierce night actions around the Solomons.

Right: This jocular cartoon conceals the narrow margin between victory and defeat at Midway.

Far right: The initial stages of the Battle of Leyte Gulf.

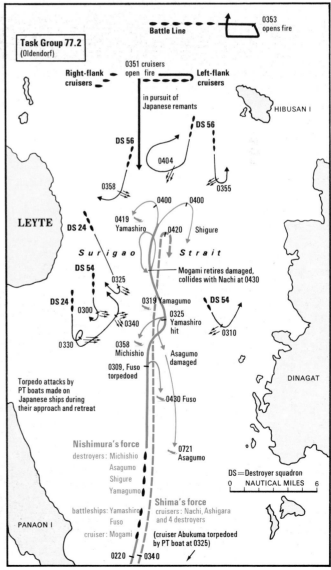

Task Group 77.2 (Oldendorf)

0353 opens fire

Battle Line

0351 cruisers open fire

Right-flank cruisers

Left-flank cruisers

HIBUSAN I

in pursuit of Japanese remnants

DS 56

DS 56

0404

0355

0358

0400 0400

LEYTE

DS 24

0419 Yamashiro

0420 Shigure

Surigao Strait

DS 54

Mogami retires damaged, collides with Nachi at 0430

0325

DS 24

0319 Yamagumo

DS 54

0300

0325 Yamashiro hit

0310

0340

0330

0358 Michishio

Asagumo damaged

0309, Fuso torpedoed

DINAGAT

Torpedo attacks by PT boats made on Japanese ships during their approach and retreat

0430 Fuso

Nishimura's force

0721 Asagumo

destroyers: Michishio Asagumo Shigure Yamagumo

DS = Destroyer squadron

0 NAUTICAL MILES 6

Shima's force

battleships: Yamashiro Fuso

cruisers: Nachi, Ashigara and 4 destroyers

cruiser: Mogami

(cruiser Abukuma torpedoed by PT boat at 0325)

PANAON I

0220 0340

5. USS Enterprise

Under the Washington Naval Disarmament Treaty of 1922 the United States Navy was limited to 135,000 tons (standard) of aircraft carriers. After the 36,000-ton *Lexington* and *Saratoga* had been converted from cancelled battlecruiser hulls the 14,500-ton *Ranger* was built. Building two more 19,000-tonners was proposed next, rather than repeating the *Ranger* design, for that small carrier was regarded as deficient in protection and speed. A larger hull was needed to accommodate more powerful machinery and better protection. In spite of this the draft design retained many features of the *Ranger*, including a flush deck with folding funnels at the edge of the flight deck. The hangars were built up as a light superstructure, not an integral part of the hull, and their sides were closed off by roller shutters. This enabled supplies and stores to be loaded easily, and the through draft of air allowed aircraft engines to be run in the hangar.

As the design developed the starboard island superstructure was enlarged to enclose the boiler uptakes, and allowed a less-cramped arrangement of the machinery than before. The boiler rooms were ahead of the engine rooms, permitting an easier method of arranging the uptakes. The extra size also allowed for better protection, with a 2½- to 4-inch belt of armor along the waterline, 4-inch bulkheads and 1½-inch armor over the machinery

and magazines. An armored hangar and flight deck were proposed at one stage, but they were ruled out because of the inroads they would make on hangar size.

The flight deck was built of 6-inch wood planking, with three aircraft lifts, two on the centerline and one offset to starboard just abaft the 'island.' Two catapults were flush-fitted at the forward end of the flight deck, but for the first time a third catapult was provided on the forward hangar deck. It was positioned athwartships, where it could launch aircraft on either beam, the purpose being to speed up the launch of a full strike without the need to have every aircraft on the flight deck.

In theory the air group would comprise 18 F2F fighters, 36 TBD dive-bombers, 37 dive-bombers and five general-purpose aircraft – 96 in all. In practice 80 was the usual aircraft complement. To meet navy requirements that aircraft could land on the flight deck from either end, two sets of arrester wires were provided, nine wires aft and four forward. The advantages of this arrangement were largely theoretical; to land on over the bow it was necessary for the carrier to steam backward, and as this method was hardly ever used in wartime the extra wires were soon removed.

The armament was heavy, eight single 5-inch guns disposed in pairs at the four corners of the flight deck. Backing them up for close-range

Far left: Launch of the *Enterprise* at Newport News in October 1936.

Left: Prewar insignia of the aircraft carrier USS *Enterprise* (CV-6).

Below: SBD Dauntless dive-bombers of VS-6 flying over the *Enterprise* barely six weeks before the attack on Pearl Harbor.

defense were to be four quadruple 1.1-inch guns, but these were not ready until after the outbreak of war.

Part of the impetus to build the new carriers was the need to provide employment, and so the two carriers were ordered together and laid down close together, *Yorktown* (CV-5) in May 1934 and *Enterprise* (CV-6) the following July. The Newport News shipyard launched the *Enterprise* in October 1936 and on 12 May 1938 she was commissioned.

When war broke out she was stationed at Pearl Harbor with the Pacific Fleet but, like the *Lexington* and *Saratoga*, she missed the Japanese onslaught on 7 December as Admiral Halsey had taken Task Force Eight (TF8) to sea some days earlier to work

the aircrews up to full efficiency. The *Lexington* also left harbor on 4 December, and as the *Saratoga* was also absent it was the battleships which took the full brunt of the Japanese attack. It has been said that this was a blessing in disguise, for without the slow battleships to form the core of the battle force the Pacific Fleet was forced into using the carriers as the spearhead of, rather than in support of, conventional fleet operations.

Although the *Enterprise* tried to find the Japanese carriers during the attack, no contact was made and she returned to the devastated base on 8 December. First attempts to strike back were ill-co-ordinated and achieved little. Apart from a risky sweep against submarines around Hawaii, the first

First Carrier Striking Force (Nagumo)
carriers: Akagi, Kaga, Hiryu, Soryu.
Second Fleet -later
2 battleships, 5 cruisers,
8 destroyers, 1 small carrier.

0430, 4 June, 1942
Air strike on Midway
launched

0534
Sighted by
US aircraft

0710-0730

Midway based
aircraft attack

0755-0839

0837
carriers begin recovering
Midway strike force

0510, 5 June
Hiryu scuttled
sinks about 0900

2400

1700
Hiryu hit by aircraft
from Enterprise

1445, Hiryu sighted

1550

1331

Hiryu launches strikes
on US carriers

1245

1100

1125
Akagi stops. Nagumo
transfers to Nagara

1913, Soryu

1925, Kaga

0500 5 June
Akagi
scuttled

1025-1030
Kaga, Akagi and Soryu hit by aircraft
from Yorktown and Enterprise

0928, US carrier borne aircraft attack
(no damage)

0918
Nagumo turns north to
intercept US task forces

TF 17 (Fletcher)
carrier: Yorktown;
2 cruisers, 5 destroyers

0430, 4 June, 1942
search and strike
patrols launched

0656

Strike force
launched

0830

0900

0752

1205-1215 and 1430
Hiryu's planes score
hits on Yorktown

1110

Strike force
sets off

0806

1500
Yorktown abandoned
sinks
0501, 7 June

1205

1430

1057

1530

1907

TF 16 (Spruance)
carriers: Enterprise, Hornet;
6 cruisers, 9 destroyers

0   NAUTICAL MILES   60

↓ Midway 50 miles

offensive action was a strike against Marcus Island in March 1942. In April, as part of Task Group 16.1, she covered her sister *Hornet* when she launched the Doolittle raid on Tokyo, but as a result both carriers missed the Coral Sea battle. They returned to Pearl Harbor on 9 May, a day too late, but ferried a Marine Corps fighter squadron to New Caledonia. On 17 May she was ordered to return at top speed, for cryptanalysts had deciphered Japanese messages confirming the attack on Midway.

The two carriers were the only forces available to stop the Japanese, unless the *Yorktown*'s serious damage from the Coral Sea battle could be repaired. Although her battle damage was estimated to need 90 days' work she sailed in three days, with a scratch air group. With Halsey in hospital with boils, command was given to Rear Admiral Fletcher, flying his flag in the *Yorktown*. He was supported by Rear Admiral Raymond A Spruance, commanding Task Force 16, with the *Enterprise* and *Hornet*.

The carriers were positioned northeast of Midway until the Japanese were sighted. The *Enterprise* launched a full-strength attack at 0700 hours on 4 June – 33 SBD dive-bombers, 14 TBD Devastator torpedo-bombers and an escort of 10 F4F Wildcats. When the torpedo-bombers arrived at the expected position of the carriers the pilots were dismayed to find that there were no targets – the sighting report was 40 miles out. When they did find the Japanese carriers their attacks were held off by gunfire and the Japanese fighters, and only four out of the 41 aircraft survived, with no hits to show for the sacrifice.

At this juncture the 33 dive-bombers from the *Enterprise* arrived over the target, and with the defenders distracted they had a clear run. At 1026 hours the first bomb hit the *Akagi*, followed almost

Right: The USS *Enterprise* in mid-1941.

Below right: SBD ready for takeoff from the *Enterprise.*

Far left: Rear Admiral Frank 'Jack' Fletcher USN, who flew his flag in the *Yorktown* at Midway.

Left: Enterprise was part of TF 16 at Midway.

Below: Oerlikon 20mm gunners of the *Enterprise* exercising off Hawaii in March 1942.

Left: Scout planes and dive-bombers ranged on the flight deck of the *Enterprise* for the raid on the Marcus Islands in March 1942.

Above: Machinist Donald E Runyon in the cockpit of his F-4F Wildcat fighter, part of VF-6 embarked in the *Enterprise.*

Above right: Vice Admiral Thomas Kinkaid (left) and Lieutenant General Walter Krueger watching the Leyte Gulf landings in October 1944.

immediately by hits on the *Kaga*. Both carriers erupted in flame. Then it was the turn of the *Soryu* to be pounded by a dive-bomber strike from the *Yorktown* and she too was devastated by explosions. Total American losses in the attack were one F-4F, 14 SBDs and 10 TBDs from the *Enterprise*, 27 aircraft from the *Hornet* and 15 from the *Yorktown*.

There was still the *Hiryu* unaccounted for, and at 1040 hours she flew off a strike of six fighters and 18 dive-bombers against the *Yorktown*. Three of their bombs set the carrier on fire, causing Admiral Fletcher to shift his flag to a cruiser at 1315 hours, leaving Admiral Spruance in charge of the carrier operations. At 1530 hours the American carriers launched their last strike, 14 SBDs from the *Enterprise* and 10 from the *Yorktown*, and they hit the Japanese carrier just as she was trying to launch a strike of her own.

Midway marked the beginning of the end for the Imperial Japanese Navy, for the skilled aircrews of the four carriers were never replaced, and the rest of the naval aircrews were squandered in operations in support of land operations. The Allies were also finding their feet after six months of unbroken Japanese victories, and two months after Midway the first major offensive was launched, an American landing on Guadalcanal in the Solomon Islands. *Enterprise* formed part of Task Force 61 under Vice Admiral Fletcher, and her air

group helped defend against massive Japanese counterstrikes. At dawn on 23 August 1942 the *Enterprise, Saratoga* and *Wasp* were in position about 100 miles east of the Solomons, waiting for a Japanese force consisting of three carriers, three battleships, 10 cruisers, 22 destroyers and a seaplane carrier. The Japanese were covering a reinforcement convoy carrying 1500 troops bound for Guadalcanal, and the carriers *Shokaku, Zuikaku* and *Ryujo* mustered between them 168 planes, as against 256 in the US carriers.

The ensuing Battle of the Eastern Solomons was a welcome victory. US carrier strikes succeeded in sinking the light carrier *Ryujo* shortly after 1400 hours, but just over three hours later the Japanese counterstrike hit the *Enterprise*. At 1714 hours a bomb hit the forward elevator and exploded below the hangar, killing 35 men and starting serious fires. Another bomb exploded in a gun position, killing 39 and setting fire to ready-use ammunition. A third bomb struck the flight deck just abaft the island, blowing a large hole in the deck.

The ship was badly damaged but could still steam, and was unlikely to sink. After an hour fires were brought under control and the flight deck was repaired sufficiently to start recovering aircraft, but suddenly her rudder jammed. At this moment 36 aircraft from the *Shokaku* and *Zuikaku* were hunting for her, but American luck held and they missed her by 50 miles.

After helping to frustrate the Japanese landing, the battered carrier made her way back to Pearl Harbor for repairs. By October she was back in the Solomons, the flagship of Task Force 16 under Rear Admiral Kinkaid. In the Battle of Santa Cruz at the end of October she was again damaged. On 26 October, the second day of the battle, she was

Above: Bomb damage to the *Enterprise*'s flight deck, received in the Eastern Solomons in August 1942.

Left: Damage to the 5-inch gun gallery on the starboard quarter of the *Enterprise*, suffered on 23 August 1942 in the Eastern Solomons.

Top right: TBF Avenger torpedo-bombers warming up aboard the *Enterprise* in May 1944, with an F-4F coming up on the elevator.

Right: A burning F-6F-3 is dealt with by firefighters aboard the USS *Enterprise*, November 1943.

hit again by a bomb on the forward flight deck, and although it went through the overhang and burst in the water, splinters inflicted damage and started a fire. A second bomb exploded inside the ship and started serious fires. A near-miss opened one of the fuel tanks, and shook the machinery. The carrier *Hornet* was sunk, making the battle a tactical victory for the Japanese. The big carrier *Shokaku* and the light carrier *Zuiho* had been seriously damaged, but the damaged USS *Enterprise* was now the only American carrier in the Pacific.

The ship put into Noumea in New Caledonia, where the repair ship *Vulcan* worked a near-miracle by getting her back to sea in 11 days. On 13 November her aircraft sank the battleship *Hiei* off Savo Island during the first phase of the Battle of Guadalcanal. Next day her air group inflicted severe damage on another reinforcement convoy, sinking six transports and damaging several escorting warships.

The arrival in the Pacific of the British carrier *Victorious* in May 1943 allowed the 'Big E' to go home for major repairs and an overhaul, and she spent 10 weeks at Pearl Harbor. For the remainder of the year she took part in a number of strikes against Japanese outposts. Under Rear Admiral Arthur W Radford the Northern Carrier Group (Task Group 50.2) hit Makin in November, and then she and the new *Yorktown* attacked shipping at Kwajalein Atoll.

On 6 January 1944 Task Force 50 became Task Force 58, the day that Rear Admiral Marc A Mitscher took command. This powerful striking force, with six fleet carriers and six light carriers, was the spearhead of a new drive into the Central Pacific. Its first raid destroyed the air defenses of Kwajalein as a prelude to the invasion of the Marshall Islands. On 17 February TF 58 raided the 'impregnable' fortress of Truk in the Caroline Islands. That night *Enterprise* launched the first night attack ever attempted by the US Navy, a dozen radar-equipped TBF Avengers. They accounted for about a third of the damage inflicted on the shipping in Truk harbor; ironically this night raid was more successful than the morning's attacks, and Truk effectively was knocked out as a main fleet base.

In the Battle of the Philippine Sea on 19 June 1944 it was an Avenger from the *Enterprise* which first sighted the Japanese Combined Fleet, and her aircraft took part in the headlong pursuit of Admiral Ozawa's carriers. The recovery of the massive strike after darkness had fallen became a nightmare. Aboard *Enterprise* the first plane to land, an SB2C Helldiver fired her 20mm cannon accidentally as she touched down. Then an SBD Dauntless just missed the Helldiver. Another Dauntless, one of the *Lexington*'s, missed all the arresting wires, bounced over the barrier and hit the island. The only other casualty was an Avenger, whose undercarriage collapsed.

On 26 August Task Force 58 became Task Force 38, with the Fifth Fleet transferred to Admiral Halsey's command as the Third Fleet. *Enterprise* and *Franklin* attacked Vice Admiral Nishimura's force in Surigao Strait during the titanic battle for Leyte Gulf in October. During the aftermath of the battle *Enterprise*'s Task Group 38.4 maintained a patrol off Leyte, and on 30 October *Enterprise* encountered her first *kamikaze*, which passed about 15 feet over the flight deck, which was packed with planes.

Early in January 1945 the Third Fleet entered the South China Sea to strike at shipping in Indochina. After sinking no fewer than 46 ships in one day (12 January) and destroying 114 aircraft the task force turned north to avoid a typhoon and headed for the Philippines and then Formosa (Taiwan). On 21 January Avengers from the *Enterprise* launched another night attack on the northern tip of the island. The sum total of the operation was the destruction of Japanese airpower in Formosa.

After a brief respite at Ulithi, Task Force 38 was reorganized, with *Enterprise* and the veteran *Saratoga* forming Task Group 58.5 under Rear Admiral Gardner. The entire force, numbering 116 warships, left the lagoon on 10 February to rehearse the Iwo Jima landings, followed by the real thing a week later. The two old carriers provided fighter cover over the island and aerial observers for the naval bombardments. When the 'Sara' was badly damaged by bomb-hits and *kamikazes* the *Enterprise* stood by the small escort carriers, whose planes were engaged in direct support of the troops ashore. Her radar-equipped aircraft enabled her air group to maintain a combat air patrol in the air for 174 hours without a break.

Despite all that the *Enterprise* had been through, her sternest ordeal was yet to come. While operating off Kyushu on 14 March she was hit by a 'dud' bomb, but the full weight of the attack was directed

Above far left: How the *New York Times* saw the Battle of Leyte Gulf. Recriminations came later.

Above: The Landing Signals Officer (LSO) brings a Hellcat in to land aboard the *Enterprise* in March 1945.

Right: A blazing Japanese attacker cartwheels into the sea over the US carrier task force off Saipan in June 1944.

USS Enterprise

Above: Admiral William F Halsey (left), Secretary of the Navy Frank Knox, and Chief of Naval Operations Admiral Ernest J King.

Below: The weary 'Big E' makes her way back to the United States two months after the end of the war.

Right: The USS *Enterprise* arrives in New York on 17 October 1945 to a tumultuous welcome.

at the *Franklin*. On the afternoon of 20 March she was bombed and strafed, but the only damage she suffered was from 'friendly' 5-inch shells fired by nearby ships; several men were killed and a serious gasoline fire was started among two parked Hellcats. A *kamikaze* attempted to dive into the inferno but its bomb missed by a few yards. The antiaircraft gunners shot down another pair of attackers, and fire parties gradually brought the fires under control.

The fierce fighting around Okinawa kept the *Enterprise* fully occupied but she did not suffer any damage until 11 April. Shortly after she rejoined Task Force 58 she was hit by a 'Judy.' This caused minor damage, but an hour later another 'Judy' hit her again. Wreckage struck the flight deck and set fire to a plane on the starboard catapult. With great presence of mind the catapult officer fired the flaming remains into the sea. The ship returned to Ulithi for repairs, but she was back in action two days later.

On the morning of 14 May the carrier force was attacked by 26 Japanese planes. The combat air patrol shot down 19 and the defending AA gunners got another six but the survivor crashed on the *Enterprise*'s forward flight deck, just abaft the forward elevator. The bomb underneath the *kamikaze*'s belly penetrated deep into the ship's vitals before exploding. With her forward elevator blown out of its well and a fire raging in the hangar she looked as if she had suffered mortal damage, but her indomitable damage-control parties got the fires under control in only half an hour. Miraculously the *Enterprise*'s casualties were compara-

tively light: 13 dead and 64 wounded.

It was the end of the war for the 'Big E.' Two days later she was sent to Ulithi, where her damage was assessed as too great for the forward-base facilities. She began the long haul to Pearl Harbor; although repaired she was never operational again. Late in September she embarked some 1100 personnel for the 'Magic Carpet' repatriation scheme. After a short conversion in an East Coast yard she went on to do two more 'Magic Carpet' trips, bringing GIs back from England.

The veteran carrier was decommissioned on 17 February 1947 and remained in reserve despite being reclassified as a support carrier (CVS) in 1953.

The battle record of the USS *Enterprise* was unequalled by any other carrier. Out of 22 possible Battle Stars awarded for the Pacific campaigns she had won 20, and she seemed a natural candidate for preservation as a war memorial. Strenuous efforts were made to save her but the time was not ripe for ship preservation, and on 1 July 1958 she was finally sold for scrap.

Although outclassed by the magnificent *Essex* Class, the design of the *Enterprise* and her sisters exemplified all the basic concepts which came to fruition in the later carriers. Despite being built within the constraints of the international treaties they achieved an admirable compromise of a large air group, good endurance and an impressive resistance to battle damage. She and her sisters were the backbone of the US carrier fleet in 1942, and the Americans' ultimate victory over Japan could not have been achieved without them.

6. HMS Sheffield

The best-known group of British cruisers in World War II were the eight 'Town' Class, and of these HMS *Sheffield* became the most famous. The 'Shiny Sheff' was involved in every major naval action in the European theater, and she served for 30 years, almost a record for a modern warship.

To understand why the Royal Navy built the 'Town' Class it is only necessary to look at the story of the *Mogami*. In 1933 the British learned that the Imperial Japanese navy intended to build a new class of cruiser displacing 8500 tons and armed with the astounding total of 15 6.1-inch guns. The Intelligence reports also suggested 5-inch side armor and a speed well over 30 knots. The Director of Naval Construction was immediately asked to prepare a comparable design, but the DNC reported that such a combination of qualities was impossible to build on such a small displacement.

What the DNC did put forward was a suggested set of characteristics which *could* be achieved, and

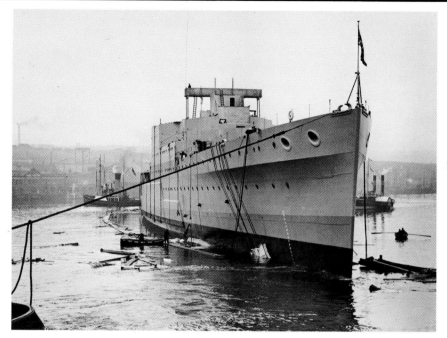

Above left: The launching of the *Sheffield* on the Tyne on 24 July 1936.

Left: The *Southampton* was the first of the 'Town' Class, built as a reply to the Japanese *Mogami* Class.

Above: HMS *Newcastle*, sister of the *Sheffield*, at Plymouth in 1938.

in September 1933 these were embodied in a new 'Staff Requirement': 12 6-inch guns in triple turrets, armored against 6-inch gunfire and capable of 30 knots at standard displacement. From this bare outline evolved a design with better armor protection, slightly more speed and enhanced antiaircraft armament. Inevitably the alterations pushed displacement up from the original target of 8500 tons, and when the design was finalized early in 1934 the standard displacement had risen to 9100 tons.

The first two ships were ordered under the 1933 Estimates, and after a brief flirtation with mythological names, they became the *Southampton* and *Newcastle*, reviving popular World War I names. The name *Sheffield* was given to one of three more ordered under the 1934 Estimates, and three of slightly improved design were ordered the following year. The keel of *Sheffield* was laid at Vickers-Armstrong's yard on the Tyne in March 1935; her launch followed in July the following year and she was completed in August 1937.

As she took her name from a comparatively modern industrial city which had not been honored in this way before, the dignitaries of Sheffield took great pride in the new cruiser. The Master Cutlers of Sheffield presented the wardroom with a stainless-steel table service in place of the traditional silver, and as a special decoration a strip of stain-

less steel was added at the deck-edge. This emphasis on stainless steel, the city's stock-in-trade, led to the ship's nickname, the 'Shiny Sheff' and she never lost her reputation for being 'smart' and well-kept.

In 1939 she was part of the 2nd Cruiser Squadron in the Home Fleet, but at the outbreak of war she became part of the 18th Cruiser Squadron and went with the capital ships and carriers to the remote base at Scapa Flow in the Orkneys. In the first month she had a narrow escape from damage. While the Home Fleet was covering the withdrawal of a damaged submarine, German aircraft attacked the *Sheffield* and the smaller cruiser *Aurora*, but all the bombs missed. It was the period known to the newspapers as the Phony War but during that time the battleship *Royal Oak* had been torpedoed inside the supposedly secure anchorage in Scapa Flow. During the dreary winter months patrolling the Denmark Strait to stop German commerce-raiders from getting out into the Atlantic there was a constant risk of battle with opponents of considerably greater fighting power.

As a unit of the Home Fleet *Sheffield* was engaged in the ill-conceived campaign in Norway in the spring of 1940, and on 30 April she and three other cruisers, six destroyers and a troop transport were sent to Aandalsnes to evacuate the 3000 soldiers still defending the town against German attacks. They succeeded in rescuing over 2000 under cover of darkness. The big ships of the Home Fleet could play no part in the evacuation of forces from France in May and June, but they provided the essential cover which prevented any attempt by the German surface fleet to interfere with the operation. Immediately afterward all naval forces in home waters were alerted to prevent the expected invasion of southern England, Operation Sealion. As part of the anti-invasion measures the *Sheffield*, her sister *Manchester* and the heavy cruiser *York* were sent from Rosyth to the Nore Command, based on Chatham and Sheerness in the Thames estuary.

Once the threat of invasion receded it was possible to send reinforcements to the Mediterranean, where Admiral Cunningham's fleet faced, on paper at least, overwhelming odds. On 22 August 1940 the *Sheffield* escorted the new carrier *Illustrious* to join Admiral Somerville's Force 'H' at Gibraltar. There she was to remain, in a team made up of the carrier *Ark Royal* and the battlecruiser *Renown*, a 'troubleshooting' force capable of reinforcing the Mediterranean Fleet or the Home Fleet at short notice.

Somerville's force provided cover for the convoys reinforcing Malta, and for the Fleet Air Arm attack on Taranto. On 25 November she and Force 'H' met the Italian battlefleet off Cape Spartivento but the ensuing engagement was indecisive as the Italian admiral took care to avoid close action with what he believed to be superior forces. The skirmish did, however, confirm both Cunningham and Somerville in their belief that aggressive tactics would keep the Italian threat under control.

What this meant in practice was demonstrated in February 1941. After a brief period escorting a convoy through the Mediterranean, Force 'H' made a cleverly disguised raid into the Gulf of Genoa. In company with the capital ships *Renown* and *Malaya* and the *Ark Royal*, the *Sheffield* bombarded Genoa, then Leghorn and La Spezia. Complete surprise was achieved and the force returned to Gibraltar without suffering a single casualty.

On 30 March 1941 in company with four destroyers she tried to intercept a French convoy making for Nemours in Algeria, but got drawn within range of shore batteries. During this action the cruiser was dive-bombed by a single French aircraft, which dropped several 250kg bombs without hitting, although minor damage was caused by blast and splinters.

As soon as the news of the *Bismarck*'s breakout was learned Force 'H' weighed anchor and headed for the South Western Approaches. As the massive air and sea search developed the initiative became more and more crucial, for the *Ark Royal, Renown* and *Sheffield* were heading for waters through which the German battleship must pass to reach a French harbor. In fact they were ideally placed for

Left: The Sheffield at speed in the spring of 1941, following the Renown and Ark Royal.

Right: Sheffield late in 1941, painted in a multicolor camouflage scheme.

Below: The carrier Ark Royal, seen with the battlecruiser Renown, was frequently in company with the Sheffield as the core of Force 'H.'

Below right: Vice Admiral Sir James Somerville (right), commanding Force 'H' and Captain Maund of the Ark Royal.

an interception by the evening of 26 May.

Earlier that day a Catalina flying boat had finally relocated the *Bismarck*, and two of the *Ark Royal*'s Swordfish torpedo-bombers confirmed the quarry's position. At 1450 hours a strike of 14 Swordfish was flown off, and an hour later, following radar contacts, they swooped to the attack through thick cloud. Unfortunately they had found the *Sheffield*, shadowing the real *Bismarck* some 20 miles away. Realizing what had happened, the cruiser held her fire and took avoiding action, but she was helped considerably by the fact that the majority of the torpedoes appeared to explode as they hit the water. They were in fact fitted with a magnetic firing pistol, and in the very heavy seas running the torpedoes were running too deep, causing the earth's magnetic field to set off the sensitive firing device.

The unhappy naval pilots were slightly comforted by a cheerful lamp signal from the *Sheffield*, and flashed back, 'Sorry for the kippers,' but a second signal to the carrier reporting the torpedo problems was vitally important. Realizing the

cause of the problem, the armorers altered the setting on the next set of torpedoes from 'noncontact' to 'contact,' so that the second strike of Swordfish, 15 aircraft launched at 1910 hours, would not make the same mistake. This time they flew to the *Sheffield*, which then gave them fresh directions to steer them toward their target.

The strike was, as we know, decisive in crippling the *Bismarck*'s steering but the *Sheffield* played no further part in her destruction. However on 12 June she played a major role in the epilogue, by sinking the tanker *Friedrich Breme*, one of 12 supply ships sent out in advance of the breakout.

The *Sheffield* was one of five cruisers escorting the 'Halberd' convoy to Malta in September 1941. Like 'Excess' in January and 'Substance' in July, massive escorts were needed to fight comparatively small groups of merchant ships through, but at a cost of one cruiser and a destroyer sunk, and a battleship, two cruisers and two destroyers damaged no fewer than 38 transports reached Malta. From June 1941 there were additional pressures to send convoys to North Russia, and for the rest of

HMS Sheffield

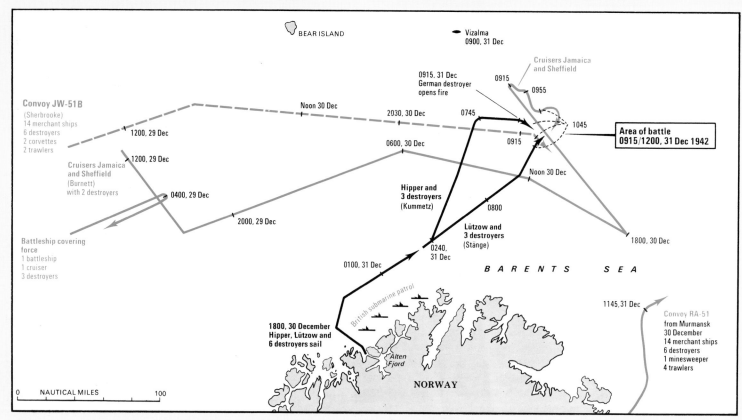

BEAR ISLAND

Vizalma
0900, 31 Dec

Convoy JW-51B
(Sherbrooke)
14 merchant ships
6 destroyers
2 corvettes
2 trawlers

Noon 30 Dec

2030, 30 Dec

0915, 31 Dec
German destroyer
opens fire

0915

Cruisers Jamaica
and Sheffield

0955

0745

1045

1200, 29 Dec

Cruisers Jamaica
and Sheffield
(Burnett)
with 2 destroyers

1200, 29 Dec

0600, 30 Dec

0915

**Area of battle
0915/1200, 31 Dec 1942**

0400, 29 Dec

Noon 30 Dec

Battleship covering
force
1 battleship
1 cruiser
3 destroyers

2000, 29 Dec

**Hipper and
3 destroyers**
(Kummetz)

0800

**Lützow and
3 destroyers**
(Stange)

0240,
31 Dec

1800, 30 Dec

0100, 31 Dec

B A R E N T S   S E A

British submarine patrol

1145, 31 Dec

**1800, 30 December
Hipper, Lützow and
6 destroyers sail**

Alten
Fjord

NORWAY

Convoy RA-51
from Murmansk
30 December
14 merchant ships
6 destroyers
1 minesweeper
4 trawlers

0   NAUTICAL MILES   100

1941 until early in March 1942 the *Sheffield* was one of a large number of warships detached to cover these vital but vulnerable convoys.

On 4 March, while escorting an Arctic convoy, she was damaged by a mine off Iceland. The mine exploded under the port quarter, blowing a 22-foot by 2-foot hole in the outer plating and inflicting severe internal damage between the keel and the decks above. The steering gear and the pumps for both after 6-inch turrets were knocked out and all electrical circuits in the vicinity were destroyed. With speed reduced to six knots she was sent back to the United Kingdom for a 17-week repair and overhaul on the Tyne. When she emerged on 11 July she had been given more radar sets to improve her air defense.

The arduous and dangerous Arctic convoys continued to occupy the ship through to the end of February 1943, but the period was not without its moments of danger. In November 1942 she was detached from the Home Fleet to cover the Torch landings in North Africa, but she afterward returned to the Home Fleet. On 31 December she took part in one of the decisive naval actions of the war, the Barents Sea Action.

Convoy JW.51B had been attacked by the *Panzerschiff Lützow* (ex-*Deutschland*) and the heavy cruiser *Admiral Hipper*. The convoy's close escort, a force of six destroyers and five smaller warships, took heavy punishment while preventing the German ships from getting to the merchant ships. The distant escort was made up of HMS *Sheffield*, flying the flag of Admiral Robert Burnett, and the slightly smaller *Jamaica*, tracking the convoy from a position about 30 miles north of the

Left: A map of the Barents Sea Action.

Right: Injured prisoners from the German oiler *Friedrich Breme* are brought aboard the *Sheffield*.

Below: The *Sheffield* in a heavy swell, escorting the Torch convoy to North Africa in November 1942.

Top: Admiral Kummetz, who led the unsuccessful attack on convoy JW.51B in December 1942.

Above: Admiral Robert Burnett flew his flag in the *Sheffield* during the Barents Sea action.

Left: The captain of the *Friedrich Breme* under interrogation aboard the *Sheffield*.

convoy. In the bad weather and gloom of the Arctic winter visibility was poor at all times, and radar played a vital role in what followed.

At about 0930 hours the two cruisers sighted gun flashes to the south, but only after another 15 minutes was Burnett certain that German surface units were on the scene. Nine minutes later they hauled round to a fresh course and increased speed to 25 knots, and then to 31 knots.

The two cruisers finally sighted the enemy at 1130 hours and opened fire on the *Admiral Hipper* at a distance of about seven miles. A 6-inch hit soon reduced the German cruiser's speed to 28 knots,

followed by two more hits as she turned away. In full chase Burnett's ships got to within 8000 yards, but snow squalls saved the *Hipper* from destruction. At 1143 hours two German destroyers suddenly blundered into the action, at a range of only 4000 yards. The *Friedrich Eckholdt* was quickly reduced to a shambles by 6-inch broadsides from the *Sheffield*, but the *Jamaica*'s target managed to escape into the gloom.

One more brief engagement took place at about 1230 hours but the German Admiral Kummetz had had enough, and was withdrawing to the west at high speed. Burnett finally called off the pursuit

HMS Sheffield

at 1400 hours, and then swept southward to guard against any attempt to get at the convoy again.

Some idea of the severity of the Arctic winter can be gauged from the fact that the *Sheffield* was badly damaged by a giant wave. At the end of February 1943, while escorting convoy JW.53 the roof of one of her forward 6-inch gun turrets was smashed in. As she was being continually swept by green seas the turrets were trained on the beam to prevent water from finding its way through the gunports. Suddenly a huge wave heaped itself against the side of 'A' turret, bending it inward and literally squeezing the armored roof clean off. The great sheet of steel fortunately fell clear of the ship into the sea.

Repairs took until early June, when she sailed from the Clyde. After a short spell in home waters she went to the Mediterranean to support the Salerno landings in September 1943, and then returned in December. Almost immediately she was involved in another Arctic convoy battle, the Battle of the North Cape.

Once again a German surface force was at sea trying to destroy a convoy carrying war material to the north Russian port of Murmansk, but this time it was the 32,000-ton battle-cruiser *Scharnhorst*. In response to pleas from Admiral Dönitz the Führer had given permission for one more major effort, and Admiral Bey had high hopes of achieving success.

Times were changing, and the British had many aces up their sleeve. Most important, they were reading German signal traffic, and so could strip the escort of a homeward-bound convoy to reinforce the outward convoy JW.55B, knowing which convoy had been sighted by *Luftwaffe* aircraft. There was also the priceless asset of radar, now perfected to the point where a battle could be fought entirely on radar contacts. This time the distant escort was reinforced by a battleship, the Home Fleet flagship HMS *Duke of York*, and if she could be brought into action her 14-inch guns would outrange the *Scharnhorst*'s 11-inch.

The cruiser escort was still under command of Admiral 'Bob' Burnett, but this time *Sheffield* had the heavy cruiser *Norfolk* and the 6-inch cruiser *Belfast* in company. As in the Barents Sea action a year before, visibility was very bad and the ships were ploughing through heavy seas. There was understandable confusion as to the whereabouts of the German ship, but at 0840 hours the *Belfast* detected a large target on her radar, at a range of about seven-and-a-half miles. Just before 0930 hours lookouts on the bridge of the *Sheffield* had their first sight of the *Scharnhorst*, and the three cruisers opened fire with starshell to illuminate the target.

The *Scharnhorst* was taken completely by surprise. An 8-inch shell burst in her control top, destroying her forward radar set, and a 6-inch shell burst on the forecastle soon after. She was nevertheless able to break away, using maximum speed to outstrip the smaller cruisers.

To Burnett it was most frustrating, for the *Duke*

Above left: A giant 50-foot wave seems about to overwhelm the 10,000-ton *Sheffield* during an Arctic storm. One such wave tore the roof off a 6-inch gun turret.

Above: The battle-cruiser *Scharnhorst*, finally brought to bay in the Battle of the North Cape.

Right: The hull of the 'Shiny Sheff' being cut up for scrap in 1968.

of York was still 200 miles away, but just after midday the *Scharnhorst* was detected once again on radar. Fifteen minutes later the cruisers opened fire on her and destroyers were ordered to attack with torpedoes.

German gunnery was better this time. The *Norfolk* was hit by two 11-inch shells without suffering any damage in return. Once more she turned away, this time heading for home, but this time Bey had decided to abandon the mission.

The delay was fatal for the Commander in Chief, Admiral Fraser, aboard the *Duke of York*, was now close enough to bring the *Scharnhorst* to battle. At 1650 hours the 14-inch guns spoke out for the first time, and once again the *Scharnhorst* was taken by surprise, being hit by the first two salvoes. Hauling around to the north Captain Hintze found the *Belfast* and *Norfolk* waiting. Finally after a long stern-chase destroyers slowed the battle-cruiser down and the *Duke of York* pounded her with 14-inch gunfire, but the *coup de grâce* was administered by the cruisers *Belfast* and *Jamaica*, whose torpedoes sent her to the bottom.

The remainder of *Sheffield's* war service was almost an anticlimax. Between January and July 1944 she continued to cover Arctic convoys and took part in various operations to neutralize the *Tirpitz*, the last German capital ship, now reduced to a fugitive existence in Norwegian fjords. The cruiser was showing signs of the hard driving she had suffered in four years of war, and in July she crossed the Atlantic for a refit in Boston Navy Yard. The overhaul was comprehensive, 'X' triple turret was removed to provide space for extra light antiaircraft guns. The ship returned to Portsmouth in May 1945, where the refit was continued until the following year.

Like other British cruisers of the period, *Sheffield* was kept busy on overseas stations, and with the Home Fleet. The Admiralty planned to modernize the five surviving 'Town' Class (*Southampton*, *Gloucester* and *Manchester* had been sunk in 1941–2) but they were halfway through their effective lives by the late 1940s, and funds were short.

The sad truth was that the *Sheffield* and her sisters had been worked very hard and their air defense was noticeably weak against anything but a second-line threat. Only massive and expensive modernization would make them fit for front-line service. Nevertheless the prestige of such ships and the power of their 6-inch guns for gunfire support made them useful for the peacekeeping mission.

The *Sheffield*, like her sisters *Newcastle* and *Birmingham*, was given a big facelift in the 1950s, with new secondary fire control, updated antiaircraft armament and a covered bridge. She served out the rest of her days without further alterations, and in 1967 she was finally sold for scrapping. An attempt to preserve her as a World War II memorial failed, but an appeal three years later to save her near-sister *Belfast* succeeded.

7. HMS Illustrious

The British Government finally awoke to the need for rearmament to meet the growing threat from Nazi Germany. In the fateful year of 1936 a massive shipbuilding program, the largest since World War I, was announced. The major items in this program, which were intended to be ready for the war which the Admiralty believed would start by the beginning of 1940, were two battleships, two aircraft carriers and seven cruisers.

At first it was planned to make the carriers repeats of the *Ark Royal*, slightly enlarged to take advantage of the international treaty limit of 23,000 tons. At the insistence of the Controller of the Navy, Sir Reginald Henderson (responsible for procurement of materiel), this design was rejected in favor of a totally new concept, an armored carrier. Previous carriers had been protected by vertical side armor and a lightly armored floor to the hangar, but Henderson proposed to armor the flight deck and its sides in order to provide greater protection to the aircraft against bombing.

The technical problems were immense; the massive topweight of 3-inch armor at such a height above the waterline could only be offset by sacrificing one hangar deck (*Ark Royal*, like contemporary US and Japanese carriers had two hangars). Even with that saving the Director of Naval Construction and his design team had to adopt numerous weight-saving devices to keep the size of the new carrier from exceeding the international treaty limit.

Finally at the end of 1936 the time came to invite tenders for the two carriers, and the names *Illustrious* and *Victorious* were selected. Both were ordered in April 1937, to be ready in three years.

Above left: The launch of the *Illustrious* at Barrow-in-Furness on 5 April 1939.

Above: One of the two Swordfish torpedo-bombers shot down during the Taranto raid being recovered by the Italians.

Above right: A Swordfish taking off from the *Illustrious*, with the *Eagle* astern.

Below right: The attack on Taranto.

Below: Illustrious shortly after completion, with Swordfish parked forward.

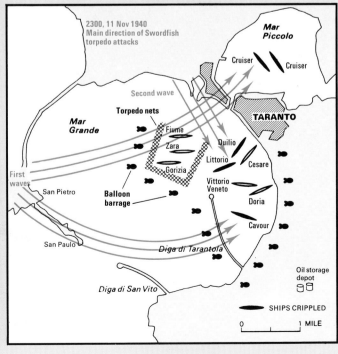

2300, 11 Nov 1940
Main direction of Swordfish
torpedo attacks

Mar
Piccolo

Cruiser   Cruiser

Second wave

Torpedo nets

Mar
Grande   Fiume

Zara   Quilio

Gorizia   Littorio   Cesare

First
waves

San Pietro   Vittorio
                     Veneto

Balloon   Doria
barrage

San Paulo   Cavour

Diga di Tarantola

TARANTO

Oil storage
depot

Diga di San Vito

SHIPS CRIPPLED

0   1 MILE

The *Illustrious* left her builder's yard at Barrow-in-Furness in April 1940, three months behind schedule, and a month later was officially accepted into naval service. Her flying trials were also conducted in great haste (a single day to test arrester wires and catapult) and after some final modifications she was ready to start her shakedown by 21 June.

The greatest drawback of Henderson's concept of an armored box hangar was the reduction in numbers of aircraft which could be carried. It was, however, logical at the time, if the extremely poor quality of British naval aircraft is considered. Thanks to nearly two decades of Royal Air Force control over the design and procurement of aircraft the Royal Navy's Fleet Air Arm was the only naval air arm in the world using biplane attack aircraft, the Swordfish and its successor, the Albacore. Nor did the Fulmar fleet fighter compare favorably with its contemporaries in speed and maneuverability. Henderson envisioned the *Illustrious* Class as 'striking down' the aircraft into the armored hangar for safety during an air attack, rather than using the Fulmar fighters to defend the ship. Defense of the ship would be left to her high-angle guns, while the aircraft sheltered from bomb fragments inside the hangar. It was a negative approach to the problem of carrier operations, but with only 21 Swordfish and a mixed fighter group of three Fulmars, four Skua dive-bombers and two obsolescent Roc fighters available for HMS *Illustrious* in mid-1940, Henderson's ideas seemed to make sense.

With her month-long shakedown cruise over, the *Illustrious* headed for the Mediterranean to reinforce Admiral Cunningham's Mediterranean Fleet, which now faced the numerically superior Italian fleet. After covering a convoy of reinforcements for the island fortress of Malta the fleet headed for a strike against the Dodecanese Islands. Cunningham noted with satisfaction the contribution made by his new carrier; the Fulmars shot down two Italian shadowers and a bomber and damaged two more, while the strike by Swordfish against the island of Rhodes achieved success, at a cost of four aircraft.

During the next two months the *Illustrious* and the older *Eagle* provided invaluable air cover as Cunningham established superiority over the Italians across the Mediterranean. In November she started preparing for Operation Judgement, which, it was hoped, would be a knockout blow against the Italian Fleet in its main base at Taranto. Using the unique night-flying capabilities of the carriers' Swordfish aircrews (the Fleet Air Arm was the only naval air service to exercise night-flying in the days before radar), Cunningham hoped to take the Italians by surprise and cripple the surface fleet.

The plan worked brilliantly. Although HMS *Eagle* could not take part, her most experienced aircrews and eight torpedo-bombers were trans-

HMS Illustrious

Far right: The scene on the after flight deck of the *Illustrious* after the Stukas' attack in Malta. The wrecked after elevator can be seen, with smoke pouring from a large hole in the deck.

Right: Captain Denis Boyd DSC RN, captain of the *Illustrious* in 1940-1.

ferred to the *Illustrious*, and the total force was increased to 24 Swordfish. Three of these were lost before the operation, but even so the total of 21 Swordfish, 14 Fulmars and four Sea Gladiator biplane fighters embarked for the attack was the largest air group so far seen aboard the *Illustrious*.

The torpedo-bombers took off in two waves on the night of 11–12 November 1940. The first wave ran into heavy antiaircraft fire, but co-ordination was excellent, with dive-bombing against subsidiary targets to divert the gunners' attention and flares dropped to illuminate the anchorage. The torpedo-bombers found their targets, and two 18-inch torpedoes hit the new battleship *Littorio*, while a third hit the older battleship *Conte di Cavour*.

An hour later the second wave arrived on the scene; their torpedoes hit the *Littorio* a third time and hit another battleship, the *Duilio*. The subsidiary attacks were also successful, as oil storage tanks were set on fire and the seaplane base was wrecked.

The impact of the Taranto raid was enormous. At a cost of only two aircraft and one crewman, and an expenditure of eleven torpedoes the *Illustrious*'s air group had eliminated half the Italian battlefleet. The *Conte di Cavour* never returned to service, and the *Littorio* and *Duilio* were out of action for months. The remaining Italian heavy units had to be withdrawn to more northerly ports and, at a crucial time in the Mediterranean, the pressure was taken off the British. The destruction of the seaplane base also freed Cunningham's ships from constant surveillance. Malta could now be reinforced without risk, and the initiative had quite clearly passed to the Mediterranean Fleet.

In desperation the Italians turned to their German allies for help, and the Luftwaffe's Fliegerkorps X, its only unit trained in antishipping operations, was sent to Sicily. The *Illustrious* was the

Below: A stoker inspecting the oil flame in one of HMS *Illustrious'* boilers.

Below right: Illustrious in December 1942 in the Indian Ocean.

target, and all training was orientated toward her destruction. On 10 January 1941 they found her just after midday, covering a convoy bound for Alexandria. A diversion by two Italian torpedo-bombers drew off the Fulmar fighters, and neither the combat air patrol nor the four fighters on deck had time to get up to 12,000 feet to disrupt the attacks of the Ju-87 Stuka dive-bombers.

Within 10 minutes the carrier was hit by six bombs, three forward and three aft. The hits forward did little serious damage, but the three aft hit the after elevator and started major fires in the hangar. With numerous casualties and her steering machinery knocked out the carrier could only steer on her engines as she dodged further bombs and tried to make her escape to Malta. She was saved by her armored deck, which restricted the worst damage to the hangar. Her main machinery was still running and she was still watertight, so as soon as the steering machinery was repaired she worked up to 18 knots. Conditions in the engine-rooms and stokeholds were almost unbearable, with thick smoke and fumes threatening to asphyxiate personnel working there.

The *Illustrious* was still on fire when she docked in Malta's Grand Harbour late that night. Her ordeal was not over, for while the dockyard patched her up for the long journey to Alexandria, Italian and German bombers tried to inflict further damage. After 13 days of nearly continous daylight bombing she slipped out to sea without being detected, and headed eastward at 23 knots.

The damage to the ship was too severe for the limited dockyard resources of Alexandria, and the US Navy was asked to undertake full repairs. The ship passed through the Suez Canal in March 1941 and reached Norfolk, Virginia, on 12 May, four months after the attack. Working at high pressure the Navy Yard succeeded in rebuilding the after part of the ship in six months, and at the same time considerable improvements were made to her equipment.

On her return to England just before Christmas 1941 she started to work up her new air group, but all plans were disrupted by the news of Japan's spectacular victories in the Indian Ocean. On 23 March 1942 *Illustrious* left to take part in the capture of Madagascar, Operation Ironclad. With her later sister *Indomitable* she provided cover for the landings at Diego Suarez, shooting down seven Vichy French aircraft and sinking an armed merchant cruiser and two submarines.

In mid-January 1943, after a comparatively uneventful spell in the Indian Ocean, *Illustrious* underwent a four-month refit before joining the Home Fleet. This tour of duty lasted less than a month, and on 5 August she sailed for the Mediterranean to replace the damaged *Indomitable* in Force H.

It was 31 months since the *Illustrious* had left Malta, but the circumstances had changed dramatically. Now the Allies were on the offensive, and having captured Sicily were trying to knock Italy out of the war. HMS *Illustrious* and her sister *Formidable* were given the task of providing fighter cover for the amphibious landings at Salerno. In three days, 9–11 September, her air group flew 214 sorties without suffering a single deck-landing

accident. Heavy Luftwaffe attacks were beaten off by antiaircraft gunfire from the two carriers and their escorting battleships *Nelson* and *Rodney*. During this period the ship's air group was increased to 50 aircraft, including 18 Grumman Martlets, 10 Seafire fighters and 12 Barracuda torpedo-bombers.

After another refit on the Clyde the carrier left early in January 1944, bound for Gibraltar on her way to join the Eastern Fleet. With the Mediterranean now firmly under Allied control she passed through the Suez Canal and reached Trincomalee in Ceylon (now Sri Lanka) at the end of the month. In March she began a series of joint operations with the USS *Saratoga*, and on 19 April the two carriers attacked Sabang at the northern end of Sumatra. The Japanese were taken by surprise and none of the attackers was shot down, but it provided the untried British aircrews with much needed experience.

Attacks on Soerabaya in Java and Port Blair in the Andaman Islands followed in May and June, and in July Sabang was raided again. This time the air group was covering a bombardment by the battleships of the Eastern Fleet. Eight Japanese aircraft were shot down and some 300 15-inch shells were fired.

The *Illustrious* then went to Durban in South Africa for a two-month refit to remedy the recurring defects which were to be her permanent scars from her ordeal in January 1941, but by the time her air group rejoined in mid-December 1944 they

were trained to a high degree. The slow and short-ranged Barracuda bomber had been replaced by the American Avenger and, with two squadrons of 18 Corsairs each, her complement reached a new high of 57 aircraft.

The first operation was a strike against the oil refinery at Palembang in Sumatra, but it needed a second attack by other carriers to inflict serious damage. *Illustrious* was soon on her way to Sydney for repairs to her machinery. She was urgently needed for the amphibious assault on Okinawa and sailed early in March 1945. As part of Task Force 57 (the designation of the British Pacific Fleet), the role of the *Illustrious* was to neutralize the airfields in the Sakishima Gunto group of islands, 200 miles away from Okinawa.

As the attacks started it became clear that the Japanese defenders were now prepared for any sacrifice to defend the Home Islands. On 1 April the first *kamikaze* attacks began. Several US carriers were badly hit, and now the British armored-deck carriers came into their own. An attacker bounced off *Indefatigable*'s deck on 1 April, and five days later heavy gunfire from the *Illustrious* deflected a Judy bomber into the water alongside. Although shaken by underwater blast the carrier was able to take part in a two-day strike against Formosa (Taiwan) four days later, before departing for Leyte.

Inspection at Leyte showed *Illustrious* had suffered serious damage. Not only was the outer plating split, but also internal frames were cracked

Left: A troop convoy heading for the landings in Madagascar in 1942.

Right: Hellcats (formerly known in British service as Martlets) warming up on *Illustrious'* flight deck before a raid on Sumatra.

Below: Troops come ashore at Salerno under cover of smoke screens.

on both sides, and her speed was accordingly restricted to 19 knots. After a short call at Sydney *Illustrious* was ordered home; she left at the end of May. When the Japanese surrendered on 15 August the war-weary carrier was undergoing repair for a further tour of duty in the Far East, but plans were immediately deferred.

When the *Illustrious* re-emerged in June 1946 she was a very different ship. The entire forward part of the flight deck had been remodelled, a new catapult was fitted, fuel stowage was increased by 30 percent and the close-range armament had been modernized. However, the deep-seated damage to her machinery could not be eradicated, and there was no question of her returning to front-line duties. Her new role was to serve as a trials and training carrier, evaluating new aircraft types and giving trainees experience in deck-landing. Except for a short break in 1948, she remained in home waters between mid-1947 and the end of 1954, providing invaluable training for the Fleet Air Arm.

In 1951 she was used to ferry troops to Cyprus, and in September 1952 she took part in her last operational cruise, when she joined in the big NATO Exercise Mainbrace. In December 1954, after one more training cruise, the old carrier steamed to the Gareloch, on the Clyde, where she was decommissioned and laid up in reserve. Her hull and machinery, although only 14 years old, were clearly worn out and she was not considered worth modernizing. In November 1956 she was sold for scrap, bringing to an end one of the most

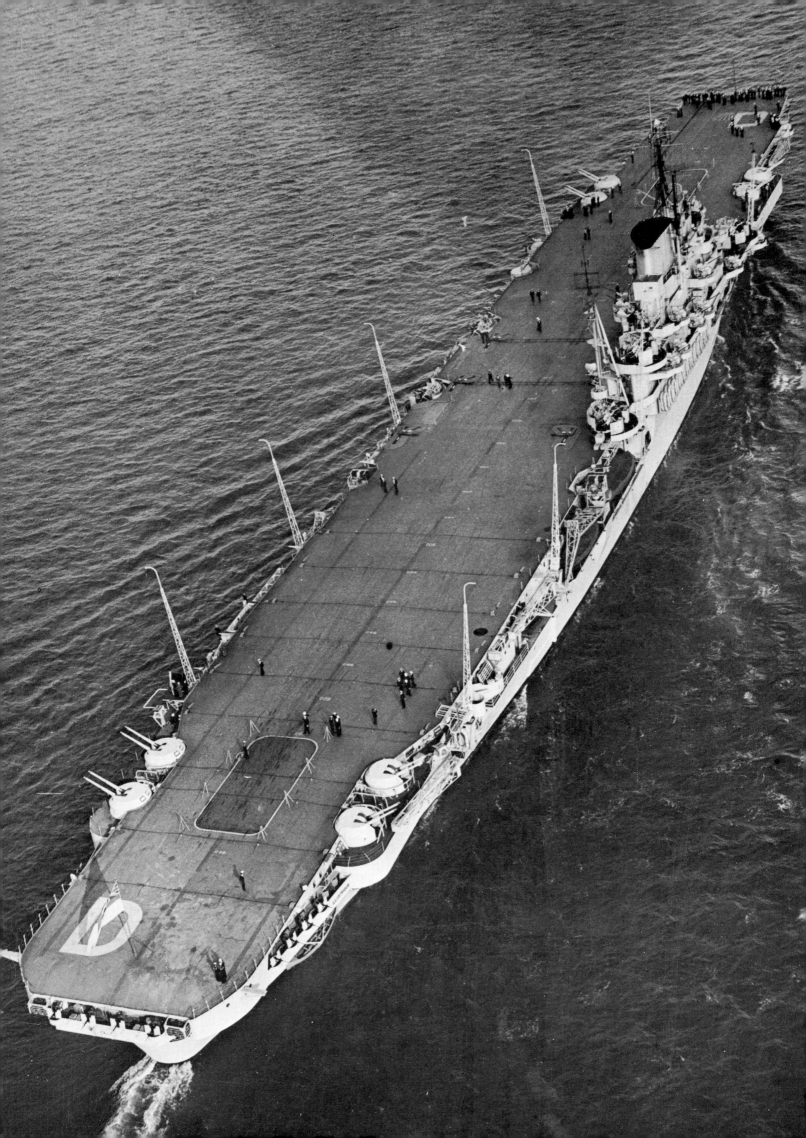

Left: Illustrious in September 1948, no longer a front-line carrier but testing new aircraft, including the first carrier jets.

Top: The 'batsman' or Landing Signals Officer giving guidance on angle and attitude to a pilot about to land on the Illustrious.

Above: A fighter landing on board the Illustrious, toward the end of her career.

distinguished careers of a World War II warship.

In retrospect the design of the *Illustrious* was only a partial success. Although, as previously pointed out, to accommodate an armored box hangar within a nominal limit of 23,000 tons was a great credit to the British designers, it can be argued that they wasted their time. War experience was to show that a properly trained, equipped and deployed air group was the main armament of a carrier, with antiaircraft guns a last-ditch defense.

The armored hangar concept of Sir Reginald Henderson went directly against this philosophy; it enshrined an older concept which treated the aircraft as ancillary to the ship. True, his design embodied a strong defensive armament, which was equally essential for carriers opposing land-based air forces, but an air group designed to number no more than 36 aircraft was too small. On the other hand, certain basic British concepts reinforced the tendency toward small air groups. The Admiralty's tough line on fire precautions had long since led to the concept of a 'closed' hangar, which provided good protection against fires but encroached on hangar space. The American and Japanese designs favored 'open' hangars, with hangar sides open, but capable of being closed by roller shutters.

Battle experience showed up the virtues and vices of both systems. The armored deck undoubtedly saved HMS *Illustrious* in 1941, although a bigger and better equipped air group could have prevented her from being exposed to such a weight of attack. The fierce engagements of the Okinawa campaign in 1945 showed that armored flight decks could be put back into fighting trim faster than the American wooden flight decks, but it can also be argued that the superior fire precautions in the British carriers helped to prevent them from being gutted by fire, as a number of US Navy carriers were. However, British carriers compared badly with their American counterparts in other respects. The US Navy had better aircraft, a superior flight deck and hangar organization and much bigger air groups. The perennial British tendency to 'think small' resulted in an ingenious 23,000-ton design, whereas the Americans could afford to wait until the expiry of international treaties permitted the building of the 27,000-ton *Essex* Class.

Whatever the truth is, both the Americans and the Japanese paid the *Illustrious* design the compliment of copying its main feature. Since 1944–5 all large US carriers have incorporated armored flight decks. During the late stages of World War II it was suggested that the Royal Navy should hand over all six of the *Illustrious* type in exchange for six *Essex* Class. This interesting mutual abandonment of cherished principles never took place, but it testifies to the merits of the British design.

Thanks to her unique combination of design qualities and her decisive contribution to some of the Royal Navy's most fiercely fought campaigns, the *Illustrious* bears the proudest name of all British carriers.

8. Yamato

In 1934 the Japanese began work on a design for a new super-battleship which would flagrantly violate the terms of the Washington Treaty. Recognizing that the industrial might of the United States could outbuild Japan very easily if war should break out, the Japanese planned to steal a march by building ships which could compete on equal terms with any group of enemy warships.

One of the essentials was that the new battleship should outrange any ship afloat or likely to be built, and she should also be impervious to any bomb or shell likely to be thrown at her. Thus the armament was to be 18-inch guns, armor was to be up to 24.8 inches thick and speed was to be 31 knots.

Not surprisingly this specification proved impossible, even to the Japanese designers, who were allowed to reduce speed to 27 knots. Much thought was given to the design, and to increase endurance a combined steam and diesel plant was suggested. Then it was discovered that the diesels selected had a major design fault, and at the last minute an all-steam plant was substituted.

The design which was emerging displaced over 64,000 tons. This was nearly twice the displacement

permitted for capital ships under the Washington Treaty, but with peculiarly Japanese logic it was reckoned that the ships would not be completed until the expiry of the various treaties. As Japan had no intention of signing the 1936 treaty, she was obliged only to declare her refusal to be bound by tonnage limits. What cannot be explained away by such semantics is the public declaration made by the Japanese Government that the new ships would have 16-inch guns, a deliberate lie to mislead the United States and Great Britain.

Another consideration in the Japanese decision to go for such a massive breach of international agreements was an obsessive desire to offset the United States' possession of the Panama Canal. Not least among the various reasons for building 64,000-ton ships was the certainty that any battleships built in reply would be too wide for the Panama Canal. Throughout the 1930s there was talk in the USA of widening the locks to take bigger ships, and if the money could be found it was hoped to start work in 1940 (such work has never been carried out). By going to such a large size the Japanese could comfort themselves that any comparable American battleship would not be able to use the widened locks either.

Below: Admiral Chuichi Nagumo led the raid on Pearl Harbor.

Bottom: The *Yamato* in the final stages of fitting-out in September 1941. Note the enormous size of her 18-inch guns.

Top: The *Yamato* hits rough weather during her sea trials in October 1941.

Above: The Japanese aimed at absolute superiority in every class of warship, from the *Yamato* Class down to destroyers.

Above right: Admiral Isoroku Yamamoto, C in C of the Imperial Japanese navy until shot down off New Guinea in April 1943.

The guns were in fact 18-inch caliber monsters, weighing 157 tons apiece and firing a 3220-pound shell a maximum distance of 45,000 yards. Each triple turret weighed 2730 tons, more than the displacement of a contemporary destroyer. Trials showed that the muzzle blast inflicted damage to nearby structures, and could literally kill exposed personnel. Special blast-proof mountings had to be devised for the antiaircraft guns, another complexity in the design process brought about by the sheer scale of the design. Each 18-inch gun fired a round every 90 seconds.

The secondary armament was also on a large scale, consisting of four triple 6.1-inch turrets. These guns were removed from the *Mogami* Class when they were upgunned to heavy cruisers, and they fired a 123-pound shell up to a maximum of

fifty-five degrees elevation.

As the ship was intended to withstand the heaviest attacks much thought had to be given to the system of protection. All boilers, turbines and auxiliary machinery were placed in individual compartments, and there were 1147 watertight compartments, of which 1065 were below the armor deck. There was a triple bottom for most of the length, to protect against mine damage. Extensive use was made of electric welding and many new features were introduced to save weight without sacrificing strength. The main armor belt, 16.14 inches thick, was inclined at 20 degrees to increase its resistance, while the 9.06-inch deck armor was intended to withstand 18-inch shells at a range of 16 miles or 1000-pound bombs dropped from a height of 11,000 feet.

Yamato

To protect against diving shells there was a lower armor belt, thinning from 10.6 inches to 3.9 inches at its bottom edge, where it met a unique armored 'floor' intended to protect the magazines from torpedo damage. The heaviest armor was on the three triple 18-inch turrets: 25.6 inches on the face, 10.6 inches on the roof, and the sides varied from 9.8 to 7.4 inches.

As might be expected, the construction of four such ships under the utmost secrecy placed considerable strain on Japan's industrial resources. It is said that the demands for rope curtains to shield the building berths dislocated the fishing industry for two years, and the requirement for ultrahigh quality armor taxed the steel industry to the limit. To meet the Navy's requirements for a battle squadron which could fight as a tactical unit the interval between building each ship had to be as short as possible. Two were ordered under the 1937 Third Reinforcement Program, followed by a second pair two years later under the 1939 Fourth Reinforcement Program.

The first ship, to be named *Yamato*, was laid down at Kure Navy Yard in November 1937, and her sister *Musashi* followed at the Mitsubishi ship-yard in Nagasaki in March 1938. The third ship, *Shinano*, was laid down at Yokosuka Navy Yard in May 1940; the keel of the unnamed *Hull No 111* was laid in the berth vacated by the *Yamato* at Kure. Nor did the plans stop there; a fifth ship was projected, along with two more armed with six 19.7-inch guns apiece, and two 32,000-ton battle-cruisers.

Work proceeded rapidly on the first two ships as soon as the design was settled. The *Yamato* was launched in August 1940 and commissioned on 16 December 1941, just nine days after the attack on Pearl Harbor. The *Musashi* took to the water in

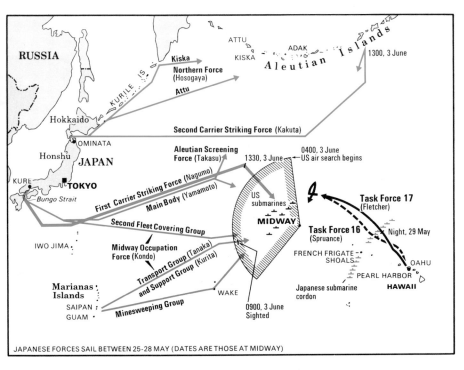

JAPANESE FORCES SAIL BETWEEN 25-28 MAY (DATES ARE THOSE AT MIDWAY)

Above left: A rare view of Yamato (left) and her sister **Musashi** together at Truk in 1943.

Left: The Musashi, second of the giants, under air attack in the Sibuyan Sea in October 1944.

Above: The Battle of Midway.

Below: The Battle of Samar, part of the Battle of Leyte Gulf.

November 1940 but was not completed until early August 1942. Work stopped on the *Shinano* and *No 111* as soon as war broke out; the former was well advanced and work was merely suspended, but *No 111* was only 30 percent complete and so the material was broken up and used for more urgent construction. Plans to build the successors died in 1942, before any work had started.

The *Yamato* joined the Battle Division on completion at the end of 1941, and inevitably became the flagship of the Combined Fleet. At Midway in June 1942 she was wearing the flag of Admiral Isoroku Yamamoto, the Commander in Chief. In that operation, codenamed MI, the battleships *Yamato*, *Nagato* and *Mutsu* formed the main body of the First Fleet, supporting Admiral Nagumo's carrier force. When the carriers were destroyed Yamamoto tried to bring his capital ships forward in the hope that they could sink the American carriers in a surface action, but they were too far away to affect the outcome, and the C in C prudently withdrew. The world's most powerful battleship force had proved impotent against a smaller force of carriers.

Although the Japanese always talked of aggressive tactics their approach to naval warfare was fundamentally cautious and defensive. The *Yamato* spent much of her time at Truk, as the flagship of the Combined Fleet. In June 1944 she was the flagship of Admiral Mineichi Koga, who had succeeded to the command on the death of Yamamoto, and when American raids on Truk became too heavy she and the rest of the fleet were removed to Tawi Tawi in Borneo.

Operation A-Go, the defense of the Marianas, followed similar lines to the Midway battle, in that the carrier force took terrible punishment without any possible help from the surface units allocated to support them. The Mobile Force Vanguard was heavily bombed by Task Force 58's carrier planes during the closing stages but the battleships were not hit, and withdrew safely.

Both super-battleships were allocated a major role in Operation SHO-1, an all-out effort to destroy the Allied amphibious landings in Leyte Gulf in the Philippines. Under Admiral Kurita, Strike Force A (comprising the *Yamato*, *Musashi* and *Nagato*, seven cruisers and nine destroyers) would lead Force B (comprising two smaller battleships, the *Kongo* and *Haruna*, five cruisers and six destroyers) through the Sibuyan Sea to attack the amphibious transports off Samar. Meanwhile the American carriers and battleships would be decoyed away by Admiral Ozawa's light carriers.

The First Strike Force sailed from Brunei Bay at 1700 hours on 22 October 1944, following a northeasterly route to avoid being detected too soon. This was a vain hope for two US submarines sighted the force and succeeded in sinking two heavy cruisers and damaging a third, while at the same time getting off a message giving the course, speed and composition of Kurita's force.

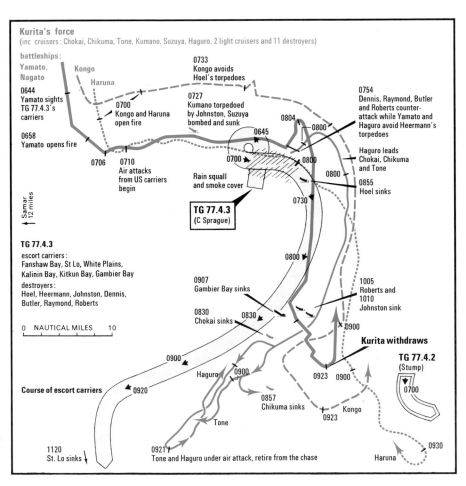

Kurita's force
(inc cruisers: Chokai, Chikuma, Tone, Kumano, Suzuya, Haguro, 2 light cruisers and 11 destroyers)

battleships:
Yamato, Nagato
Kongo
Haruna

0644 Yamato sights TG 77.4.3's carriers

0658 Yamato opens fire

0700 Kongo and Haruna open fire

0706

0710 Air attacks from US carriers begin

0727 Kumano torpedoed by Johnston, Suzuya bombed and sunk

0733 Kongo avoids Hoel's torpedoes

Rain squall and smoke cover

TG 77.4.3 (C Sprague)

0645

0700

0730

0804

0800

0800

0800

0800

0754 Dennis, Raymond, Butler and Roberts counter-attack while Yamato and Haguro avoid Heermann's torpedoes

Haguro leads Chokai, Chikuma and Tone

0855 Hoel sinks

Samar 12 miles

TG 77.4.3
escort carriers:
Fanshaw Bay, St Lo, White Plains, Kalinin Bay, Kitkun Bay, Gambier Bay
destroyers:
Hoel, Heermann, Johnston, Dennis, Butler, Raymond, Roberts

0 NAUTICAL MILES 10

0907 Gambier Bay sinks

0830 Chokai sinks

0830

0800

1005 Roberts and 1010 Johnston sink

0900

Kurita withdraws

Course of escort carriers

0900

0920

Haguro 0900

0857 Chikuma sinks

Tone

0923 0900

Kongo

0923

TG 77.4.2 (Stump)

0700

1120 St. Lo sinks

0921 Tone and Haguro under air attack, retire from the chase

0930

Haruna

Admiral Kurita, having had his flagship sunk under him, was now aboard the *Yamato*. The force entered the Sibuyan Sea at 0630 hours the next morning, but the first air raid did not begin until midmorning. In all five attacks were made, lasting until late in the afternoon. They concentrated on the *Musashi*, which took 13 torpedoes on the port side and another seven on the starboard side, as well as 17 bomb hits and 18 near-misses. Not even her massive protection and elaborate counter-flooding arrangements could cope with such damage, and as the inrush of water got out of control she settled lower and lower. Kurita left her behind, and she finally gave up the fight at 1835 hours, taking 991 of the 2279 men on board down with her.

The *Yamato* took two bomb hits at 1330 hours, but in spite of taking on 2000 tons of water her damage-control parties counterflooded and brought her back on to an even keel. Although there were no more air strikes on the way Kurita had no way of knowing this, and ordered a temporary with-

drawal at 1500 hours to keep out of range of US carrier aircraft. At 1614 hours he reversed course once more, and the force prepared to sail through the San Bernardino Strait under cover of darkness.

It is easy to imagine Kurita's surprise when his force emerged next morning to find no air raids and no hostile ships. It could hardly be credited that Admiral Halsey had not only taken the bait offered by Ozawa's decoy force but had left the Strait unguarded. To make matters worse nobody on the American side appeared to be aware what had happened and no reconnaissance aircraft had sighted Kurita's battleships.

Forces A and B turned southeast at 0540 hours, forming six columns. All that stood before them were three groups of small escort carriers, the three 'Taffies' of Task Group 77.4, with a light escort. Visibility was not good, with overcast skies, haze and occasional squalls. At 0549 hours a Japanese lookout sighted mastheads at about 28,000 yards and three minutes later Kurita ordered speed increased to 24 knots. At 0558 hours the order was

Above: US sailors cheer as a Japanese torpedo-bomber is shot down. After their initial successes Japanese aircraft scored comparatively few hits on US ships. Better co-ordinated air defense and radar-directed fire control took a heavy toll.

Above right: The *Yamato* circles under heavy air attack during her last sortie in April 1945.

Right: The *Yamato* takes a bomb hit forward of 'A' turret while passing through the Sibuyan Sea on 24 October 1944.

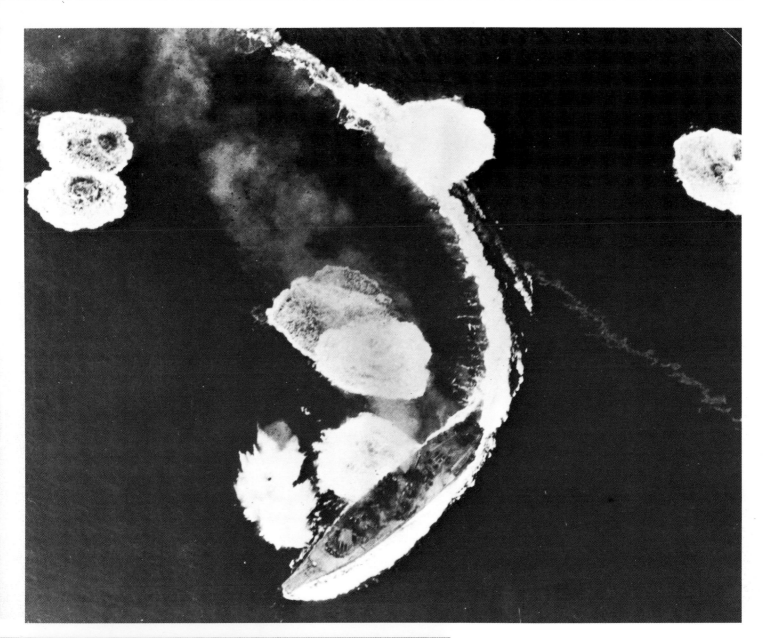

given to open fire, and for the first time *Yamato*'s 18-inch guns fired in anger.

On paper it should have been a massacre, but there were several reasons why it did not turn out that way. Not surprisingly, Kurita expected air attacks at any minute, and he also consistently overestimated the strength opposing him. For example he mistook the six 'jeep carriers' for fleet carriers. Nor did the American forces accept the situation tamely; although the carriers' planes were armed for supporting troops ashore, and in some cases had no bombs left, they flew low over Japanese ships in simulated attacks. Similarly the six destroyers and destroyer escorts laid smoke screens and made torpedo attacks.

It was a technique which the British had used against the Germans and Italians when badly out-numbered, and it worked. The battle became a mêlée, with no tactical co-ordination, and when Japanese ships began to suffer damage it lost what little cohesion it had. The carrier *Gambier Bay* was finally destroyed at 0741 hours by repeated hits from cruisers but the price was too heavy: three heavy cruisers were badly damaged, and air attacks were gaining in strength. In the poor visibility Japanese gunners were not scoring sufficient hits to destroy the opposition, and there was dwindling hope of breaking through the ring of defenders.

At 0811 Kurita signalled 'Cease action. Come north with me, 20 knots,' and the *Yamato* headed north. After a turn to the southwest (the direction of Leyte) he reversed course once more and headed for San Bernardino Strait. He had lost a battleship and five heavy cruisers, and two more had been crippled, to achieve the sinking of one small carrier and three escorts. Kurita survived the war but never gave a satisfactory explanation for his abrupt withdrawal; historians attribute it to the cumulative effects of strain under constant air attack, poor Intelligence about the rest of the battle, and finally poor health.

Although the Strike Force suffered no further loss SHO-1 was at an end, and with it went the last remnants of Japan's claim to command the sea. Part of the Combined Fleet returned to Brunei and then to Lingga Roads, off Singapore, where there was fuel but very little ammunition. Other ships returned to Japan, where there was plenty of ammunition but no fuel. The fleet that had humbled American, British and Dutch military might was now helpless.

Even without an effective fleet the Japanese showed no signs of giving up, and the 'island-hopping' campaign continued to tighten the ring around Japan. Early in 1945 the Allies landed on Iwo Jima as a prelude to the occupation of Okinawa. Okinawa was the last outpost before the home islands themselves, and when the landing started on 1 April Imperial General HQ immediately decided that every means must be used to dislodge the enemy. The day chosen, 6 April, was designated TEN-GO Day, and in addition to massive *kamikaze* attacks it was decided to use the *Yamato* on a suicide mission. The battleship was to act as a decoy, luring away as many carrier planes as possible, and leaving the Allied naval forces around Okinawa vulnerable to the *kamikazes*.

The shortage of oil was now so acute that the *Yamato* could be spared only enough to get her to Okinawa. If she succeeded in fending off the air attacks she was then to beach herself and use her 18-inch guns in support of the defending ground troops. Her escorts for this forlorn hope were to be the light cruiser *Yahagi* and the destroyers *Isokaze*, *Hamakaze*, *Yukikaze*, *Asashimo*, *Kasumi*, *Hatsushimo*, *Fuyuzuki* and *Suzutsuki*.

After putting ashore cadets and sick personnel the force left Tokuyama at 1600 hours on 6 April, heading for Okinawa. At 0400 hours next morning they emerged into the North Pacific southeast of Kyushu. At 0900 hours the *Asashimo* reported that she had engine trouble and dropped astern. The force was disposed in a circular formation, with the *Yamato* in the center.

Above: Yamato on fire after bomb hits during her last sortie.

Left: A huge pall of smoke marks the final explosion which destroyed the Yamato on 7 April 1945.

Below: The sinking of the Yamato had symbolic significance, for she represented Japanese 'invincibility' more than any other warship.

BIGGEST JAPANESE BATTLESHIP SUNK

Quarter Of Remaining Fleet Smashed

From DAVID DIVINE,
War Correspondent of "The Sunday Times"

ADM. NIMITZ'S H.Q., Saturday.
The Yamato, last of Japan's 45,000-ton, 16-inch gun battleships, and the most powerful unit in the Japanese fleet, has been sunk in a big sea-air battle with the American forces near Okinawa.

In addition, two Japanese cruisers and three destroyers were sunk and 391 Japanese planes were shot down.

An official Navy spokesman declared to-night that a good 25 per cent. of the major combat force left to Japan had been destroyed or put out of action in the battle, and that the whole of the Japanese fleet remaining "could be handled easily by any of our major task forces."

American losses were three destroyers and seven planes, with several more destroyers and some smaller craft damaged.

NEW JAPANESE CABINET

Premier Gloomy

NEW YORK, Saturday.
A Japanese News Agency broadcast reports that 77-year-old Adm. Suzuki has formed a Cabinet following the resignation of the Koiso Government 48 hours earlier. Suzuki will also hold the offices of Foreign Minister and Minister for Greater East Asia.

The new Cabinet consists of relatively unknown statesmen, and its members are a singularly un-warlike body. None of the great army figures who have been running the country for the past four years is included.

In his inaugural address the new Premier said: "The war, which is being fought for the very existence of our Empire, has come to its most important and crucial stage, and warrants not the least bit of optimism in our nation's survival. If the situation continues like this the basis of our nation's existence might be threatened. The enemy has now firmly established himself

According to a communiqué issued by Adm. Nimitz, the action began yesterday afternoon, when strong Japanese air forces attacked American ships operating off Okinawa and shore installations on the island.

It was in this action that the American losses were sustained. But no big ships were hit, and 341 of the attacking aircraft were destroyed—245 by carrier aircraft, 55 by fighters and 51 by anti-aircraft fire.

Early this morning, scout planes sighted the enemy naval force which had left the Inland Sea and, passing south of Kyushu, was entering the East China Sea. Immediately a fast carrier task force was sent to intercept it.

HIT BY 3 TORPEDOES

Carrier aircraft attacked about mid-day, in face of heavy anti-aircraft fire from the ships, but with no air opposition. The Yamato was hit by at least three torpedoes and eight heavy bombs, and sank about 50 miles south-west of Kyushu, the southern island of Japan.

In addition to the two cruisers and three destroyers sunk, three more destroyers were left burning.

Of the entire Japanese force, only three destroyers escaped, and they were heavily hit with rockets and machine-guns.

In other actions to-day, 30 Japanese planes were destroyed. The Yamato, reputed to be of at

---

The TEN-GO force turned southwest at 1115 hours and 15 minutes later an enemy floatplane was sighted. With no further need for reconnaissance the Japanese floatplanes were immediately launched and sent back to Kyushu. Soon reports were received of up to 250 aircraft heading for the force, and at 1220 hours the *Yamato* signalled that she had detected many aircraft 33,000 yards off her port bow, just before a rain squall blotted them out.

As the rain squall cleared the last battle began. At 1252 all the ships opened fire, and even the *Yamato*'s 18-inch guns joined in, firing 'splash barrages' to deter low-level attacks. The ships were still only 175 miles south of Kyushu, and there was no hope of influencing the battle for Okinawa.

The light cruiser *Yahagi* bore the brunt of the first wave of attacks. She was hit repeatedly by torpedoes and bombs, then strafed until her engine-rooms were piled high with dead. The destroyers came next, the *Hamakaze* going down quickly. The *Suzutsuki* was soon on fire, while the *Kasumi* was hit in the rudder and lost control. The battered *Yahagi* sank shortly afterward, followed by the *Isokaze*.

The first bombs hit the *Yamato* at 1240 hours and 10 minutes later torpedoes hit her on the port side. She took eight more torpedoes on the port side, followed by two on the starboard side. Progressive flooding was dealt with by the damage-control parties but soon they were overwhelmed by the volume of water; by 1405 hours the ship was no longer responding to counterflooding. 'Abandon ship' was piped, and at 1417 hours a last torpedo increased her list to 20 degrees. Finally she gave up the fight to stay afloat and as she capsized she blew up, sending a huge column of smoke billowing up thousands of feet overhead.

Survivors were taken off by the *Kasumi*. The losses were heavy: 2498 killed in the *Yamato*, 446 in the *Yahagi* and 721 in the four destroyers. Only four destroyers, the *Fuyuzuki*, *Suzutsuki*, *Yukikaze* and *Hatsushimo* limped back to Sasebo. Nor did the *kamikaze* raid on Okinawa fare any better. The 114 planes succeeded in damaging only one carrier, an old battleship and a destroyer. The Imperial Japanese Navy no longer existed.

It remains only to complete the story of the Japanese giant battleships by recalling the fate of the third ship. The giant hull of the *Shinano* lay on the stocks until June 1942, by which time it had been completed up to the main deck. The need for aircraft carriers to replace the losses at Midway led to her completion as a 68,000-ton carrier, and as such she was launched in October 1944.

The carrier was only partially completed as it had been decided to move her to the Inland Sea to protect her from air raids. While *en route* she was hit by four torpedoes from the US submarine *Archerfish*. The inexperienced crew and workmen aboard did not understand the damage-control routine, and after seven hours she capsized and sank, about 160 miles southeast of Cape Muroto.

9. Bismarck

Of all the battleships which fought in World War II, the German *Bismarck* continues to be the most fascinating to many people. Her mysterious breakout, the sinking of the British battle-cruiser *Hood*, and her subsequent pursuit and destruction have all the ingredients of high drama.

She and her sister *Tirpitz* had their origins in Hitler's deliberate flouting of the disarmament clauses of the Versailles Treaty. In secrecy the Kriegsmarine was authorized to build two 'battle-cruisers' or fast battleships of 32,000 tons, the *Scharnhorst* and *Gneisenau*. No sooner had they been publicly confirmed than the German government announced that two much bigger battleships, *Bismarck* and *Tirpitz*, would be laid down in 1935–6. Like the *Scharnhorst* and *Gneisenau*, the two ships would be even larger than their official displacement tonnage indicated: although claimed to displace 35,000 tons to conform with international agreements, the new ships would displace some 7000 tons more.

Fortunately for the British and their French allies the Kriegsmarine's ambitious plans were slow to be implemented, and the *Bismarck* was not ready for active service until April 1941, by which time new British battleships were ready. Even so,

the *Bismarck* was some 4000 tons larger (the new British ships were some 3000 tons over the Washington Treaty limit, the design having been modified at the outbreak of war), which gave the *Bismarck* an advantage in speed and protection.

On paper the German ship was impressive, and her powerful appearance confirmed that impression. She was armed with eight 38cm (15-inch) guns, mounted in four twin turrets, and in addition had powerful secondary 15cm (5.9-inch) guns and numerous light antiaircraft weapons, ranging from 10.5cm (4.1-inch) down to 2cm caliber. In many ways the design was conservative, with an armored deck placed comparatively low in the ship, where it provided excellent protection against long-range gunfire but would have been less effective against aircraft bombs. Nor was there any attempt to copy the dual-purpose high-angle/low-angle guns developed by the Americans and British for their contemporary designs, so considerable weight was wasted. After the sinking of the ship on her first and only sortie, legends were to grow about her massive protection. Even a mysterious formula for her steel armor appeared, but in fact her side belt of 12.6-inch armor was comparable to her opponents and German steel armor was no better and no worse than anybody else's.

Above: **The launch of the *Bismarck* on 14 February 1939.**

Right: **Aerial reconnaissance quickly revealed the presence of the *Bismarck* and *Prinz Eugen* in a fjord near Bergen, and soon a massive air and sea search began.**

Above: Grand Admiral Raeder, architect of Hitler's new Kriegsmarine. His plan to use surface ships in combination with U-Boats failed with the loss of the *Bismarck*.

Left: Bismarck in Hamburg early in 1941.

The British were well aware of the threat posed by the *Bismarck*. Her role was to operate as a lone commerce-raider, driving off or sinking the cruisers and destroyers covering the North Atlantic convoys, and then sinking the hapless merchant ships at will. In the face of a battleship the only defense was to scatter the convoy, and those ships which did not fall to the *Bismarck*'s guns would fall victim to U-Boats' torpedoes. As she neared the end of her trials and shakedown in the Baltic in the early weeks of 1941 the British deployed all their Intelligence resources to detect the first signs of a breakout.

On the evening of 20 May 1941 the British Naval Attache in Stockholm learned from friendly Swedes that two large ships had been seen heading from the Baltic toward the Kattegat; that night the Admiralty started the first of a series of steps to stop the breakout. Aerial reconnaissance soon detected the *Bismarck* and the 8-inch gunned heavy cruiser *Prinz Eugen* in Bergen. On 21 May the departure of the two ships was reported to the heavy cruisers HMS *Suffolk* and HMS *Norfolk*, on patrol in the most likely breakout route, the Denmark Strait between Iceland and Greenland.

The two German ships were detected on radar by HMS *Suffolk* on 23 May, but Admiralty orders

Left: The Kriegsmarine rated highly in Nazi propaganda, but the fleet was a disappointment.

Below: Bismarck firing her 15-inch (38-cm) guns during gunnery trials in the Baltic.

Bottom: The action of the *Bismarck*.

to Scapa Flow had already sent the Battle-cruiser Squadron to sea to reinforce the patrol. This force comprised the 20-year old battle-cruiser *Hood*, of approximately the same size and gunpower as the *Bismarck*, and the brand-new battleship *Prince of Wales*, smaller but more heavily armored and armed with ten 14-inch guns. By 1922 hours the same night they were southwest of Iceland, moving on a course at which they would intercept the German ships at first light.

Hydrophone operators aboard the *Prinz Eugen* detected the first trace of the *Hood* and *Prince of Wales* at 0500 hours the next morning. Vice Admiral Holland in the *Hood* had hoped to make his interception under the most favorable conditions, with his ships' full main armament available, but an undetected change of course by the Germans put his ships on a fine angle of approach, with only their forward guns able to bear on their targets. As one of the *Prince of Wales*' guns could fire only one round before jamming, this reduced the British to four 15-inch and five 14-inch guns, opposing eight 15-inch and eight 8-inch. The *Prince of Wales* had only been completed two weeks previously, and her untried gun turrets were manned by young and inexperienced crews.

In spite of these limitations the first salvoes from the *Hood* came as an unpleasant shock. With the aid of radar her fire control was accurate for distance, although off-line, and aboard the *Bismarck* it seemed that the fourth salvo might score at least one hit. But instead, as the handsome old battle-cruiser started a turn to port to bring her after guns into action, a salvo of 15-inch shells landed around her, and she vanished in a huge explosion. For a few seconds both German and British onlookers were stunned into silence as the two halves of the *Hood* vanished in a dense cloud of smoke and debris, and then the battle started afresh, with a hurricane of fire directed at the *Prince of Wales*.

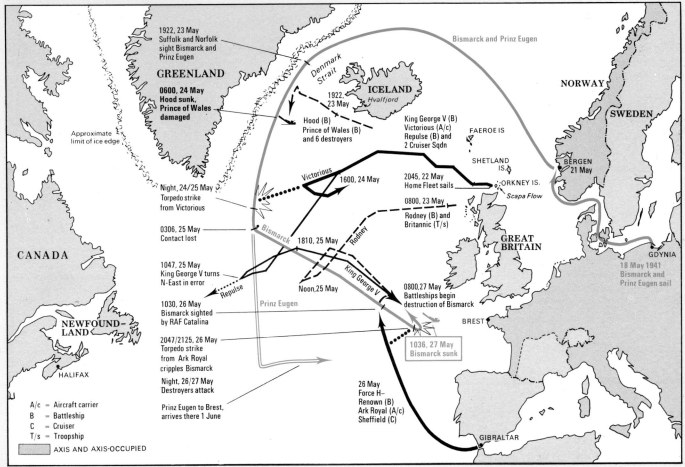

Bismarck and Prinz Eugen

GREENLAND

ICELAND
Hvalfjord

NORWAY

SWEDEN

1922, 23 May
Suffolk and Norfolk
sight Bismarck and
Prinz Eugen

Denmark
Strait

1922,
23 May

0600, 24 May
Hood sunk,
Prince of Wales
damaged

Hood (B)
Prince of Wales (B)
and 6 destroyers

King George V (B)
Victorious (A/c)
Repulse (B) and
2 Cruiser Sqdn

FAEROE IS

SHETLAND
IS.

BERGEN
21 May

Approximate
limit of ice edge

Victorious

1600, 24 May

2045, 22 May
Home Fleet sails

ORKNEY IS.
Scapa Flow

Night, 24/25 May
Torpedo strike
from Victorious

0800, 23 May

Rodney (B) and
Britannic (T/s)

0306, 25 May
Contact lost

Bismarck

1810, 25 May

Rodney

GREAT
BRITAIN

GDYNIA

CANADA

1047, 25 May
King George V turns
N-East in error

King George V

18 May 1941
Bismarck and
Prinz Eugen sail

Repulse

Noon, 25 May

0800, 27 May
Battleships begin
destruction of Bismarck

1030, 26 May
Bismarck sighted
by RAF Catalina

Prinz Eugen

NEWFOUND-
LAND

1036, 27 May
Bismarck sunk

BREST

2047/2125, 26 May
Torpedo strike
from Ark Royal
cripples Bismarck

HALIFAX

Night, 26/27 May
Destroyers attack

26 May
Force H–
Renown (B)
Ark Royal (A/c)
Sheffield (C)

Prinz Eugen to Brest,
arrives there 1 June

A/c = Aircraft carrier
B = Battleship
C = Cruiser
T/s = Troopship

AXIS AND AXIS-OCCUPIED

GIBRALTAR

Bismarck

The British ship was soon in trouble. A 15-inch shell hit the compass platform, ricochetted off the binnacle and killed or wounded everyone on the bridge except Captain Leach. In short order another six hits followed, three 15-inch and three 8-inch shells, but the ship's guns were still firing, and four straddles of 14-inch salvoes were scored against the *Bismarck*. The inexperienced crew of 'X' quadruple 14-inch turret had let a shell drop out of the loading hoist, resulting in a jammed roller-path. With a great deal of physical effort the 1400-pound shell was manhandled back into the hoist and the turret resumed firing.

Fortunately none of the other hits was as deadly as the 15-inch hit on the compass platform. Some shells detonated partially and others failed completely. Captain Leach was determined to continue the fight, but to Rear Admiral Wake Walker aboard HMS *Norfolk*, now the senior surviving officer after the death of Holland, it seemed as if the *Prince of Wales* was about to be sunk, and he ordered her to break off the action.

To the Germans it looked very similar, and they could be forgiven for thinking that they had not only sunk the pride of the Royal Navy, the 'Mighty *Hood*,' but had also forced the latest British battleship to flee with her tail between her legs. But two 14-inch shells had inflicted serious underwater damage which would ultimately lead to the sinking of their ship. The *Bismarck*'s fuel tanks had been holed, allowing sea water to contaminate a large quantity of oil fuel; this, combined with the loss of 200 tons of oil at Bergen, when a refueling hose had been damaged, seriously impaired the chances of maintaining a lengthy cruise in the North Atlantic.

To Admiral Lutjens, flying his flag in the *Bismarck*, it seemed that his squadron's remarkably cheap victory must be the prelude to an even greater victory against the North Atlantic convoys. He overruled a request from Captain Lindemann to pursue the *Prince of Wales*, but within two hours he was forced to admit that the ship must put in to a French port to repair the damage. With 2000 tons of water forward and as much as a third of her fuel contaminated the *Bismarck* could not afford to embark on a lengthy patrol in the North Atlantic. Nor had she managed to shake off her faithful shadows, the *Suffolk* and *Norfolk*, whose radar pulses could be detected, regularly generating a telltale 'blip' on a cathode ray tube. They would sooner or later guide more British heavy units to the scene, so it was imperative to sink them, or at least shake them off the scent, to allow the *Bismarck* and *Prinz Eugen* to reach nearer to the coast of France, where they could call on the Luftwaffe for air cover.

The Admiralty was indeed mobilizing every resource to hunt down the *Bismarck*, but for two days luck turned against them. First the shadowing cruisers were thrown off the scent by a clever ruse; to cover the escape of the *Prinz Eugen*, which separated from the *Bismarck* late on the 24th,

Right: Admiral Wake-Walker took command after the sinking of the *Hood* and the death of Admiral Holland.

Far right: Admiral Gunther Lutjens, who went down with his flagship.

Above: Bismarck seen from *Prinz Eugen.*

Right: At the outbreak of war HMS *Rodney* was one of the world's most powerful battleships.

Captain Lindemann turned back on the shadowers, using his 15-inch guns to drive the cruisers out of radar range. By the time they turned back the *Bismarck* was out of range of the *Suffolk*'s radar. For nearly two days the *Bismarck* was loose in the North Atlantic, with ships and aircraft hunting fruitlessly for her.

Another roll of fortune's dice was to bring German hopes to ruin. Not realizing that his flagship was out of range of HMS *Suffolk*'s radar (the radar signal could be detected aboard *Bismarck* but was too weak to reach back to the *Suffolk*), Admiral Lutjens sent a long radio message back to Germany on the 25th. Although it took some time to plot the bearings correctly, the British direction-finding stations were able to calculate the *Bis-*

marck's approximate position from the transmission, and at 1030 hours on 26 May a Catalina flying boat of the RAF sighted an enormous oil slick trailing from the *Bismarck*'s damaged fuel tanks. Now it was to be a race to stop the *Bismarck* before she reached the safety of the French coast.

The aircraft carrier *Victorious* had already tried one torpedo-bomber strike on the night of 24–25 May, but the single 18-inch torpedo which hit had not slowed the *Bismarck* down. Destroyers had also carried out a daring night attack, but with no result. The Home Fleet flagship *King George V* was closing at top speed, as was the battleship *Rodney*, and other heavy units were heading for the area, but the only heavy unit within striking distance was the carrier *Ark Royal*, which had steamed up from Gibraltar with her escorts.

After a first abortive strike, which mistook the cruiser HMS *Sheffield* for the enemy battleship, the 'Ark' launched a second strike of Swordfish torpedo-bombers. In spite of a withering fire from the *Bismarck*'s flak batteries the lumbering biplanes succeeded in hitting her twice, once on the armor belt amidships and once right aft. That second hit sealed her fate, for it wrecked the steering gear and jammed the rudders. The giant battleship careered wildly in circles until she could be slowed down to permit steering on the four propeller shafts.

The ship's divers worked through the night to try to free the rudders. At one stage it was proposed that the damaged rudders be blown away with explosive to improve the ship's steering, but by then the weather was so bad that nothing could be done. All that was left for the *Bismarck* was to steer a clumsy zigzag course like an injured crab, heading steadily for the French Atlantic coast but knowing that she must shortly prepare to sell her life as dearly as she could.

Next morning lookouts sighted the unmistakeable silhouettes of a *King George V* Class battleship and another of the *Nelson* Class. It was in fact HMS *King George V* herself, the flagship of the Home Fleet, and HMS *Rodney* – two of the Royal Navy's most powerful ships. Taking advantage of the *Bismarck*'s slow speed and erratic steering, the British C in C, Admiral Sir John Tovey, ordered his two battleships to maneuver independently, giving each ship full freedom to use maximum gunpower without masking each other's fire. Both ships lost no time in closing the range and at 0847 hours the *Rodney* opened fire with 16-inch salvoes, followed a minute later by the flagship, at a range of about 20,000 yards.

Bismarck replied with her forward turrets 'Anton' and 'Bruno' at 0849 hours, and obtained a straddle on the *Rodney* but the target suffered only splinter damage and continued inexorably to close the range to a point where even her secondary 6-inch guns were firing. After 20 minutes of concentrated fire the *Bismarck*'s main fire-control station was out of action, and the after turrets 'Caesar' and 'Dora' were firing under local control.

Bismarck

By now shells were falling everywhere, destroying communications and power supplies and inflicting fearful casualties among the gunners, signallers and searchlight operators at their stations in the superstructure. Yet the ship remained defiantly afloat, apparently immune to the 14-inch and 16-inch shells.

As intended, the low, thick armored deck was proving very resistant to heavy gunfire at intermediate ranges, and subsequent interrogation of survivors suggest that many shells were going straight through the unarmored parts of the hull without penetrating the armored deck. Admiral Tovey realized this, and ordered *Rodney* to move in to a range of about 4000 yards to inflict as much structural damage as she could, while the flagship opened the range to 14,000 yards to improve the chance of getting a plunging hit.

The plan was working, and eye-witnesses aboard HMS *Rodney* testify to seeing full broadsides of nine 16-inch shells visible in the watery May sunshine just before they crashed into the *Bismarck*'s topsides. The pride of Hitler's newly-created Kriegsmarine was methodically being shot to pieces, and the only question was, how long?

The agony of the ship and the 2200 men aboard was coming to an end. The two British battleships were running short of fuel, and the C in C ordered the heavy cruiser *Dorsetshire* to sink the blazing wreck with torpedoes. The cruiser approached the wallowing hulk on the starboard side, and fired three torpedoes. As these seemed to have no effect she steamed around to the port side and fired a fourth. At 1036 hours the *Bismarck* rolled over and sank, taking with her all but 200 of her company.

The sinking of the *Bismarck* marked a turning point in the Battle of the Atlantic. Although the smaller battleships *Scharnhorst* and *Gneisenau*

Bismarck

Previous pages: John Hamilton's portrayal of the scene from HMS *Zulu* as the British destroyers attempted a night torpedo-attack on the *Bismarck*.

Top left: 16-inch salvoes from the *Rodney* falling astern of the *Bismarck*.

Left: To counterbalance the psychological effect of the loss of the *Hood* the British press made the most of the *Bismarck* sinking.

Above: Some of the 200 *Bismarck* survivors being rescued by the heavy cruiser *Dorsetshire*. Others were picked up by U-Boats.

were soon joined in Brest by the *Prinz Eugen*, and remained a powerful 'fleet in being' it was the end of Admiral Raeder's grand design to use major surface units in conjunction with U-Boats against the convoy system. The *Bismarck*'s sister *Tirpitz* remained a thorn in the flesh of the British, but her long sojourn in Norway's fjords never put anything like the same amount of pressure on the convoy system. Even when the notorious PQ.17 convoy was given the order to scatter the *Tirpitz* left her anchorage too late to intercept the convoy, and her one great chance to affect the outcome of the naval war in Europe passed by.

The Germans blamed the disastrous outcome of Operation Rhine on treachery, and failed to recognize their mistakes. The brilliant British 'Ultra' code-breaking operation was only beginning to break into the German naval cyphers, so it cannot be given the credit for the outcome. The British spotlighted Bergen as the likely anchorage for the two ships merely by intelligent analysis of the radio-traffic patterns. Low-grade cyphers yielded information about the preparation of deep moorings, confirming the guess that two deep-draught ships would be arriving shortly. Poor Intelligence about the performance of British radars led Admiral Lutjens into making his terrible

blunder on 25 May, when he sent a long message to Germany and thereby gave away his position to the British, with dire consequences.

Lutjens has also been criticized many times for overruling Captain Lindemann's advice to return to Bergen to effect repairs to the fuel system. It is significant that independent British and American assessments of the German admiral's tactical handling of the operation came to the conclusion that his decision to press on could not be justified. It seems that Lutjens interpreted his orders from Raeder and Hitler very literally, and may even have succumbed to the propaganda about his 'unsinkable' flagship.

In retrospect it can be seen that ultimately the *Bismarck* would have been sunk, even if she had made a second sortie. The sinking of the *Hood* and the escape from the shadowing cruisers in the Denmark Strait were enormous strokes of luck, but even the damaged and half-trained *Prince of Wales* succeeded in causing sufficient damage to cause the Atlantic raiding mission to be aborted. Historically the lone commerce-raider has always proved vulnerable to battle damage, and the *Bismarck* was no exception.

What the German Navy also failed to take into account was the new factor of air power. Aerial reconnaissance proved able to locate and identify the *Bismarck* on several occasions, and even the inadequate Swordfish biplanes of the Fleet Air Arm were able to hit her with torpedoes. Had she faced an air arm of the quality of the US Navy or the Imperial Japanese Navy her sinking might have taken place three days sooner. A year later Allied air superiority in the Atlantic would have made the *Bismarck*'s sortie impossible.

The hunting of the *Bismarck* was an immensely complicated operation. Despite the loss of the *Hood* (the cause of which remains a mystery to this day) and a bad mistake by Tovey's staff in initially plotting the direction-finding 'fixes' incorrectly, the British organization had worked remarkably well. Two major units whose presence was decisive, the battleship *Rodney* and the carrier *Ark Royal*, both headed for the battle zone without waiting for orders from London. The torpedo-strike from the *Ark Royal* has become legendary, not just for the pilots' bravery in the face of the German gunfire but for their skill in taking off and landing in appalling weather conditions.

For the German Navy the short and disastrous career of the *Bismarck* had a deeper significance. By sinking the pride of the Royal Navy and subsequently going down with her battle ensign still flying the *Bismarck* had gone some way to exorcise the memory of Scapa Flow in 1919, when the High Seas Fleet had scuttled itself after a tame surrender to the Allies. Just as her building was a gesture of defiance by Hitler against the humiliations of the Versailles Treaty, her sinking expressed the wish of the Navy to prove that it could fight and win on the high seas.

10. USS New Jersey

Previous pages: The newly recommissioned *New Jersey* firing her guns in the Pacific in March 1983.

Left: The launch of the battleship *New Jersey* (BB-62) at Philadelphia on 7 December 1942.

Above: Admiral Raymond A Spruance USN, who flew his flag in the *New Jersey* from February 1944.

With the ending of the last of the naval limitation treaties in 1940 the US Navy was at last freed from the 35,000-ton limit on battleship displacement. This meant that for the first time in nearly two decades ship design could be optimized for function rather than as a series of compromises within a fixed volume.

The designers of the so-called '1940 battleships' were allowed to keep the armament of the preceding *South Dakota* Class, but as the ships would have to screen the new *Essex* Class fast aircraft carriers, their speed would have to be increased from 28 to 33 knots. This involved an enormous increase of installed power, from 77,000hp to a massive 212,000hp, and in turn dictated a much larger ship. Although the nominal displacement was 45,000 tons the new design worked out at closer to 51,000 tons when built.

The design process was not without its hitches. When the Washington Treaty put an end to the building of a series of large battleships in 1922 their 16-inch guns had been saved, and were being held in reserve for use in a future class (a considerable saving on the cost of new construction). Yet for a period of 18 months the Bureau of Ships and the Bureau of Ordnance failed to check that the barbette diameter in the new battleship design would be big enough to take a turret with three of the 16-inch guns in it. The error was discovered, and it was necessary to design and build a new lighter model of 16-inch gun. Only the vast industrial power of the United States could have reacted in such a short time. As things turned out the major problem affecting the construction of the new

battleships was the serious shortage of steel in 1942–3 occasioned by the vast construction programs of merchant ships and escorts for the Battle of the Atlantic.

Six ships were planned, the *Iowa* (BB 61), *New Jersey* (BB 62), *Missouri* (BB 63), *Wisconsin* (BB 64), *Illinois* (BB 65) and *Kentucky* (BB 66). Of these only four were completed, the *Illinois* being cancelled at the end of the war when only 22 percent complete and the *Kentucky* was suspended while plans were discussed for a possible rearming with missiles.

The *New Jersey* was launched in December 1942 at the Philadelphia Naval Shipyard and was commissioned on 23 May 1943. Her trials and shakedown were carried out in the Western Atlantic and Caribbean, but it was not until early January 1944 that she passed through the Panama Canal, bound for the Pacific Theater. She was heading for Funafuti in the Ellice Islands, where she was to join the Fifth Fleet.

The ship was soon in action; with Task Group 58.2 she took part in the assault on the Marshall Islands, screening the carrier force while they flew off strikes against Kwajalein and Eniwetok prior to the landings on 31 January. Four days later she became the flagship of the Fifth Fleet when Admiral Raymond A Spruance broke out his flag from her mainmast. Her first action as flagship was to lead an audacious strike against Truk, the supposedly impregnable bastion constructed by the Japanese in the Carolines. During the attack on 17–18 February the task force sank two light cruisers, four destroyers, three armed merchant

Below: The *Missouri,* third of the *Iowa* Class, in 1945.

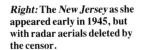

Right: The *New Jersey* as she appeared early in 1945, but with radar aerials deleted by the censor.

Below: In 1945 the battleship's main role was to screen carriers with antiaircraft gunfire. This *kamikaze* crashed on HMS *Formidable*'s flight deck.

cruisers, two submarine tenders and a number of lesser ships.

On the ship's return to Majuro, Spruance shifted his flag to the heavy cruiser *Indianapolis* but her duties remained largely unchanged. In April 1944 she screened the carriers giving air support to the invasion of northern New Guinea and then accompanied them on another raid against Truk. During the attack on Truk she shot down two torpedo-bombers and on 1 May she bombarded Ponape.

The next major operation was the assault on the Marianas, which triggered off the Battle of the Philippine Sea. On 12 June the *New Jersey*'s gunners downed a torpedo-bomber and during the next two days the 16-inch guns shelled the invasion beaches on Saipan and Tinian. On 19 June she was put into the 'gun line,' a screen protecting the carriers from Japanese aircraft. During the 'Great Marianas Turkey Shoot' the Japanese lost some 400 aircraft, many of them to the massed 5-inch, 40mm and 20mm gunfire of the battleships, all for the loss of 17 US aircraft.

After supporting strikes against Guam and the Palau Islands the ship sailed for Pearl Harbor, where on 24 August she became the flagship of Admiral William F Halsey Jr, commanding the Third Fleet. For the next eight months she was based on Ulithi, escorting the fast carriers as they ranged across the Pacific, hitting at the Philippines, at Okinawa and even as far afield as Formosa (Taiwan).

As Halsey's flagship, the *New Jersey* played an important role in the Battle of Leyte Gulf. In the opening phase the task force carriers struck at the Japanese Southern and Center Forces, sinking the battleship *Musashi* on 23 October. Things then went wrong when Halsey's staff misinterpreted signals, and the Admiral impetuously ordered his ships to pursue what turned out to be a decoy force.

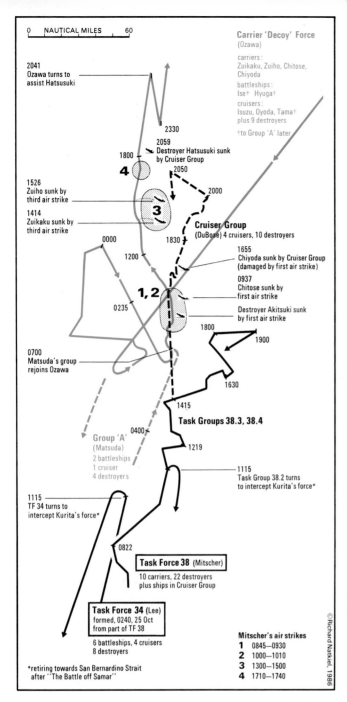

```
0 NAUTICAL MILES 60

2041
Ozawa turns to
assist Hatsusuki

2330

2059
Destroyer Hatsusuki sunk
by Cruiser Group

1800
4

2050

1526
Zuiho sunk by
third air strike

3

2000

1414
Zuikaku sunk by
third air strike

0000

1200

1830

Cruiser Group
(DuBose) 4 cruisers, 10 destroyers

1655
Chiyoda sunk by Cruiser Group
(damaged by first air strike)

0235

1, 2

0937
Chitose sunk by
first air strike

Destroyer Akitsuki sunk
by first air strike

0700
Matsuda's group
rejoins Ozawa

1800

1900

1630

1415

Task Groups 38.3, 38.4

0400

Group 'A'
(Matsuda)
2 battleships
1 cruiser
4 destroyers

1219

1115
Task Group 38.2 turns
to intercept Kurita's force*

1115
TF 34 turns to
intercept Kurita's force*

0822

Task Force 38 (Mitscher)
10 carriers, 22 destroyers
plus ships in Cruiser Group

Task Force 34 (Lee)
formed, 0240, 25 Oct
from part of TF 38

6 battleships, 4 cruisers
8 destroyers

*retiring towards San Bernardino Strait
after "The Battle off Samar"
```

Carrier 'Decoy' Force
(Ozawa)

carriers:
Zuikaku, Zuiho, Chitose,
Chiyoda

battleships:
Ise† Hyuga†

cruisers:
Isuzu, Oyoda, Tama†
plus 9 destroyers

†to Group 'A' later

Mitscher's air strikes
1 0845—0930
2 1000—1010
3 1300—1500
4 1710—1740

©Richard Natkiel, 1986

Above left: The third phase of the Battle of Leyte Gulf.

Left: The *New Jersey* was hurriedly recommissioned for the Korean War and arrived off the east coast in May 1951.

Above: The *New Jersey* docking in San Francisco Bay on 24 June 1969 on completion of a cruise off Vietnam.

Right: The *New Jersey* and her sister *Wisconsin* at Yokosuka during the Korean War.

USS New Jersey

The amphibious forces lying off Samar were now wide open to Japanese attack, and the *New Jersey* was turned southward, racing at top speed to try to avert disaster. Fortunately the attack had been defeated by the forces on the spot, and the Japanese had been driven off by the time the flagship returned.

With the Japanese main fleet destroyed the carriers could resume their strikes on central and south Luzon, but now the first *kamikaze*s appeared. For a month the battleships were heavily engaged, trying to protect the vulnerable carriers by throwing up massive barrages of antiaircraft fire. While trying to stop a *kamikaze* from hitting the carrier *Intrepid* the *New Jersey* was hit by machine-gun fire from the carrier, which wounded three men.

The battleship was again involved in defending the *Intrepid* on 25 November, and shot down a *kamikaze* attacking the light carrier *Cabot*.

While on her way back from a strike against Luzon in mid-December the *New Jersey* was caught in a typhoon which overwhelmed three destroyers. Her last cruise as Halsey's flagship took her to Formosa, Okinawa, Hong Kong and Indochina before returning to Ulithi on 25 January 1945. As the flagship of Rear Admiral Badger she now led Battleship Division Seven in the assault on Iwo Jima. In February she screened a group of carriers launching a strike against Honshu, in the Japanese home islands. Her last major operation was to cover forces softening up Okinawa for the big assault in April.

Above: The *New Jersey* emerged from retirement in 1967 for a facelift at Philadelphia Navy Yard before sailing to Vietnam.

The *New Jersey* was now in urgent need of a refit, and on 27 April she entered Puget Sound Naval Shipyard for a two-and-a-half-month overhaul before heading back to the Pacific. By the time she reached Guam and hoisted the flag of Admiral Spruance for the second time the war was over, but she remained in Japanese waters until relieved by her sister *Iowa* at the end of January 1946. For the homeward journey she embarked nearly 1000 troops, heading for San Francisco.

After a short overhaul the *New Jersey* was transferred to the Atlantic, where she joined a training squadron bound for Europe. After a successful cruise she returned to New York and became flagship of Battleship Division One, but she was soon decommissioned at Bayonne and joined the 'mothball fleet,' the New York Group of the Atlantic Reserve Fleet.

It was widely assumed that the remaining US Navy battleships would never see action again. In the shadow of the atom bomb the arguments of strategic airpower seemed compelling, and even the future of aircraft carriers was challenged. All this changed with the North Korean invasion of

South Korea, for here was a 'limited war' in which naval airpower and gunfire support were badly needed to offset enemy superiority in numbers.

The *New Jersey* was recommissioned at Bayonne on 21 November 1950 and after a brief shakedown arrived off the east coast of Korea on 17 May 1951. Three days later she fired her first 16-inch salvoes in support of the Wonsan landings. During this bombardment she received a hit from a shore battery on No 1 turret and was near-missed by a second shell; one crewman was killed and two wounded. During her six-month tour of duty the accuracy of her gunnery became a legend, with an apparently unending series of bombardments of enemy positions.

When relieved by her sister *Wisconsin* in mid-

November the *New Jersey* headed for Yokosuka, then to Hawaii and Long Beach, reaching Norfolk via the Panama Canal just before Christmas 1951. After a major overhaul lasting six months she returned to training duties, embarking NROTC midshipmen for a cruise to Cherbourg, Lisbon and back to the Caribbean.

The ship's second tour of duty in the Korean War began when she sailed from Norfolk in March 1953. The routine was as demanding as before, a continual round of direct gunfire support for hard-pressed land forces and the occasional interdiction of enemy communications far behind the front line. She was kept busy right up to the cease-fire at the end of July 1953, and remained in Korean waters until relieved three months later by the

Above: The *New Jersey* on completion of her trials in Delaware Bay in March 1968.

USS New Jersey

Inset left: Bob Hope and Ann-Margret cutting a cake aboard the New Jersey as part of a Christmas 1968 entertainment for the crew.

Inset right: The insignia of the *New Jersey*.

Below: The *New Jersey* and the carrier *Coral Sea* off Vietnam.

USS New Jersey

Wisconsin once again. In mid-October she left Yokusuka bound for Norfolk, where she resumed training duties. For two summers she took midshipmen across the Atlantic, then in September 1955 she joined the Sixth Fleet in the Mediterranean for a short spell before carrying out two more training cruises in 1956. After a last operational spell as flagship of the Second Fleet she was decommissioned and mothballed at Bayonne in August 1957.

The ship's third lease of life came about because of intense lobbying by the US Marine Corps for heavy-gun support in the Vietnam War. Alarmed by the declining number of 8-inch gunned cruisers, the Marines demanded that one of the 'battlewagons' should be brought out of reserve to meet the growing demands for gunfire support. A survey of all four mothballed *Iowa* Class showed that the *New Jersey* was in the best condition, and she was overhauled in 1967–8. To keep costs down the refit was austere, with 40mm guns removed and communications renewed, but little else done beyond refurbishment of machinery and accommodation.

Amid enormous publicity she recommissioned in April 1968 and arrived in Vietnam toward the end of September. Once again she went into the repetitive routine of shore bombardments, broken only by short visits to Subic Bay in the Philippines. In her first two months on the 'gun line' she fired over 3000 16-inch and nearly 7000 5-inch shells.

The first tour of duty ended and at the beginning of April 1969 the battleship left Subic Bay for Japan, en route to the USA. But while she was still at sea an international incident occurred; North Korean jets shot down an unarmed electronic surveillance plane, and *New Jersey* was recalled to join a newly-formed task force. She finally reached Long Beach on 5 May and started an overhaul in preparation for a second tour of duty.

While the ship was being refitted and readied for service the Department of Defense was reacting to popular dislike of the war by making a number of cosmetic cuts in the defense budget. On 22 August 1969 it was announced that the *New Jersey* and a number of other ships were to be deactivated. She left Long Beach on 3 September, heading for a lay-up berth at Puget Sound Naval Shipyard. When the colors were hauled down on 17 December many believed that the battleship era had at last come to an end.

Times were changing however, and technology came to the rescue. The US Navy had tried to win funding for a 17,000-ton nuclear cruiser design, known as the Strike Cruiser or CSGN. When the design was dropped in the 1970s proposals were put forward to provide equivalent surface firepower by rearming the *Iowa* Class with Harpoon and Tomahawk antiship missiles. The rationale of the project is to create four new large missile-armed 'platforms,' each one the core of a Surface Action Group (SAG), which can operate in conjunction

Above: The *New Jersey* firing at targets near Tuyhoa in South Vietnam, during her time on the 'gun line,' 1968-9.

Left: Docking the *New Jersey* on her return from Vietnam late in 1969.

with the 15 Carrier Battle Groups (CBGs). The presence of a large ship armed with 16 Harpoon antiship missiles and 8 Tomahawk cruise missiles will, it is argued, tie down Soviet forces which would otherwise be free to take offensive action against US and allied forces. The four battleships, with comparatively little service, were in good condition, and far cheaper than new construction.

Arguments about the vulnerability of the battleships are met by the provision of new electronic countermeasures equipment, 20mm Phalanx 'Gatling' guns for defense against missiles, and above all, screening by powerful antiaircraft and antisubmarine escorts. The sheer size of a battleship hull, with its 12.1-inch armor belt, thick deck armor and minute subdivision means that several hits by antiship missiles could be sustained without seriously disabling the ship. In the words of one officer, 'we might not be eating donuts in the wardroom but it wouldn't do much in terms of damage.'

The current worry about the battleships' role in the Surface Action Groups is no longer their vulnerability to surface or air attack, but to submarine attack. When the massive geared turbines were designed in the early 1940s little thought was given to their underwater 'noise signature.' In today's

world of AntiSubmarine Warfare (ASW) noise reduction is all-important, and ASW experts fear that the high noise levels generated by the Westinghouse turbines and the old-fashioned propellers and gearboxes will act as a 'beacon' for Soviet submarines. These fears have already been countered by the provision of towed antitorpedo decoys and some measure of shrouding the noisiest elements.

In 1980 Congress finally agreed to fund the conversion of the *New Jersey*, the most modern of the four *Iowa* Class. In July 1981 the ship was eased out of her berth at Bremerton and taken in tow to her former homeport, Long Beach. There she was completely stripped and overhauled. New radars were installed, the boilers were converted to burn distillate fuel, and four twin 5-inch gun mountings were removed to create space for the Harpoon canisters and the armored box launchers for the Tomahawks. The modernization lasted from October 1981 to Christmas Eve the following year, and she was formally recommissioned four days later by President Reagan.

The conversion of the second battleship, the USS *Iowa*, began at the Avondale Shipyards in New Orleans a year after the start of *New Jersey*'s, and she was recommissioned on 28 April 1984.

Left: Lubricating strut bearings on a propeller during the 1982 reactivation of the *New Jersey.*

Below: On 23 March 1983 the *New Jersey* fired a Harpoon antiship missile.

Inset top right: The recommissioning of the *New Jersey* on 28 December 1982 took place in the presence of President Reagan.

Inset below right: The awesome sight of a broadside of 16-inch guns, fired by the *New Jersey* off Beirut on 9 January 1984.

Above: The *Iowa*, second of
the class to be reactivated and
rearmed, fires her 16-inch
guns in the Western
Approaches to the English
Channel in September 1985.

There had been talk in the 1970s of preserving the USS *Missouri*, the 'Mighty Mo,' as a war memorial, for the unconditional surrender of Japan had been signed on board in Tokyo Bay in August 1945, but she too was to be reprieved as the third of the battleship conversions. She was towed to Long Beach Naval Shipyard and work began in May 1984; her recommissioning is planned for July this year. The fourth, *Wisconsin*, started her overhaul and conversion in October 1985 and will recommission at the start of 1988.

More ambitious plans for a Phase 2 conversion were drawn up, but the rising cost of the Phase 1 conversions will probably halt the program there. The Phase 2 plans allowed for the removal of the after triple 16-inch turret, to be replaced by a flight deck for helicopters and AV-8A or AV-8B Short TakeOff/Vertical Landing (STOVL) aircraft. This would create a ship of remarkable flexibility, capable of supporting limited war and acting as a major offensive unit in a major war. There are also plans to provide the 16-inch guns with subcaliber boosted shells, capable of reaching 50 miles, but for the moment the ships are equipped with conventional armor-piercing (AP) and high-explosive rounds, the AP rounds being useful against concrete fortifications.

The *New Jersey*'s first active-duty assignment came in August 1983, when she was ordered into the Caribbean to reinforce US anger at Nicaraguan incursions into neighboring El Salvador. Then in 1984 she was ordered to the Mediterranean to support American action against pro-Syrian factions in the Lebanon. Several shoots were carried out against artillery positions which were shelling US Marines in Beirut, the first time a US warship had fired her guns in anger in the Mediterranean for 40 years. As with all peacekeeping operations, there were many political limits and constraints on the use of military force, and the 16-inch bombardments achieved little tangible result.

In the summer of 1985 the second modernized battleship, the *Iowa*, visited Europe, and gave a vivid demonstration of firepower. As a part of a three-week NATO exercise code-named Ocean Safari the battleship was subjected to simulated missile attacks in the southwestern approaches to the British Isles, and then carried out a full-caliber firing.

The survival of the *New Jersey* and her sisters into the nuclear age is a remarkable story, and the busy career of the *New Jersey* over a period of more than 40 years even more remarkable. Regarded at one time as white elephants, the battleships have proved a much better investment than their designers and builders could ever have imagined. No other World War II warships can boast of such an extended career.

Left: The *New Jersey* now
mounts Harpoon and
Tomahawk missiles and has
20mm Phalanx 'Gatling' guns
for close-in defense against
missile attack.

Index

The publisher would like to thank Adrian Hodgkins who designed this book, Jane Laslett who edited it and Wendy Sacks who did the picture research. Special thanks to Dave McLoughlin and Chris Shuff of The Photo Source and to the agencies listed below who supplied the illustrations:

Archiv für Kunst und Geschichte: page 15 (top left).
BBC Hulton Picture Library: pages 24, 26 (both), 62 (top), 70 (top left), 77 (bottom).
Bison Picture Library: pages 49 (center and bottom), 70 (top right), 90 (top left).
Bundesarchiv: page 88.
Fleet Air Arm Museum: pages 70–1 (bottom), 99 (center).
John Frost Newspapers: pages 17, 19, 40 (bottom), 41, 58 (left), 85 (bottom), 94 (bottom).
Imperial War Museum, London: pages 1, 4–5, 8, 12–13, 18 (both), 22, 23 (bottom), 25 (bottom), 27 (top), 35 (top left and bottom), 36, 37 (bottom right), 39 (top and center), 40 (top), 43 (bottom), 64 (top), 65 (both), 66–7 (all five), 68, 69 (top), 72 (top left and top right), 73, 74–5 (all three), 82, 87 (both), 90 (bottom), 94 (top), 95, 98 (top), 98–9 (bottom).
Imperial War Museum, London/John Hamilton: pages 6–7, 7 (bottom), 92–3.
National Maritime Museum, London: pages 20 (both), 23 (top), 24–5 (top), 32–3, 39 (bottom), 63.
Richard Natkiel (maps): pages 22 (both), 27, 36 (both), 49, 52, 66, 71, 81 (both), 89, 100.
Peter Newark's Historical Pictures: pages 15 (bottom), 16–17, 43 (top), 71, 83 (top), 102 (top), 102–3, 103.
Ships of the World: pages 44–5, 48, 78 (bottom), 80 (top), 84–5.
Rolf Steinberg: page 16 (top right).
TPS: page 30 (bottom).
TPS/Central Press: pages 9, 28, 76, 91.
TPS/Fox Photos: pages 21 (both), 29, 33 (inset), 34, 37 (top and bottom left).
TPS/Keystone: pages 31, 35 (top right), 50 (left), 52 (top left), 55 (right), 59, 62 (bottom), 64–5, 69 (bottom), 72–3, 77 (top), 79 (bottom left), 90 (top right), 98 (top right), 102 (bottom).
US Naval Historical Center: pages 40–1, 42 (both), 47 (both), 79 (top and bottom right), 107.
US Navy: pages 2–3, 6 (bottom left and right), 49 (top), 53 (both), 55, 56 (both), 57 (top), 60–1 (top and bottom), 78 (top), 96–7, 100–1 (all three), 104–5 (all three), 106, 108–9, 109 (inset top and bottom), 110, 111.
US Navy/MARS, Lincs: page 108 (inset).
US Navy (National Archives): pages 44 (inset), 46 (both), 50 (inset), 51, 52–3, 54, 55 (left), 57 (bottom), 58 (right), 60 (top left), 80 (bottom), 83 (bottom), 84 (bottom), 98 (top left).
WZ Bilddienst, Wilhelmshaven: pages 10–11, 13 (top), 14–15 (top), 15 (top right), 16 (top left), 30 (top), 38–9, 86, 89.